The Law of the Offerings

Considered  rious
Aspects of t arist

ANDREW JUKES

"This is the law of the Burnt-offering, of the Meat-offering, and of the Sin-offering, and of the Trespass-offering, and of the consecrations, and of the sacrifice of the Peace-offerings."—Leviticus vii, 37.

New York   Chicago   Toronto
Fleming H. Revell Company
Publishers of Evangelical Literature

CONTENTS.

PREFACE.

HE, who spake as never man spake, opened His mouth in parables. With His example before us, I have often been surprised that the inspired parables of the Old Testament should have been so neglected; the more as we see from the writings of St Paul, not only how closely these emblems are connected with Christ, but also how aptly they illustrate, in simplest figures, the wondrous truths and profound mysteries of redemption.

Some years ago, one of these Old Testament parables was made an especial blessing to myself. This led me further; and having learnt by personal experience the preciousness of these emblematic Scriptures, I have since freely used them in ministering to others the truths connected with Christ's Work and Person. Some months since, I gave a course of Lectures on THE OFFERINGS, which were taken down in short-hand at the time. At the repeated request of others, I have since corrected them as time has allowed. They are now published in the following pages.

As to the great outlines and principles contained in them, I may say that I have confidence that they are

in the main correct : mixed with much infirmity and
weakness I doubt not ; (how much few perhaps will feel
more than I do ; indeed it has been the sense of this
which has so long delayed their publication ;) yet still
I trust according to the mind of God, and setting forth
not only a measure of truth, but also *the* truth which
the Offerings were intended to typify.   Where they
contain error, may the Lord and His saints pardon it :
where truth, may we all acknowledge it as His, and
follow it.   I need not say, "I have no commandment
of the Lord."   I merely "give my judgment as one
that hath obtained mercy of the Lord to be faithful."

It only remains for me to add here, that I have derived much assistance upon this subject from a Tract
entitled, *The Types of Leviticus.** I cannot follow
the writer of it in his view of every Offering.   I do
not know how far he would assent to the principles I
have applied to their varieties.   Yet I feel that under
God I am much his debtor, I doubt not for far more
than I am even conscious of.

I now commend these pages to the Lord.   May He
be pleased to use them, as shall seem good to Him, to
His glory.

HULL, *September* 1847.

* Published by J. K. Campbell, High Holborn.

THE TYPES IN GENERAL.

GAL. IV. 21–31.

————

"THE works of the Lord are great, sought out of all them that have pleasure therein." Such was the witness of one of old; and the saints of God can yet set their seal to it. Great, indeed, are the works of the Lord; sought out, and sought into, are they by His people: but how great, how exalted, how wondrous, none feel so deeply as those who have most considered them! Man's work, if we are continually poring over it, will soon weary us—a little attention will in time make us masters of it. God's work, the more we examine and look into it, will only attract us the more. The more it is studied, the more it opens out, at every step unfolding fresh and endless objects. Take any portion of it—the earth, the air, the sky; and the further we search, the deeper we examine, the more are we led to acknowledge that as yet we know next to nothing, and that the great ocean of truth of every kind lies before us, as yet all unfathomed and unfathomable.

The reasons for this are many. A very obvious one is that man is finite, God infinite; and the finite cannot measure the infinite. Another reason is, that God

A

uses the same instrument for many and different ends. Thus, when we know one use or end of this or that part of creation, we may yet be ignorant of many other ends which God may be carrying out by the same means. Take, for example, the air. How many ends does God accomplish by this one simple element! Air supplies the lungs, supports fire, conveys sound, reflects light, diffuses scents, gives rain, wafts ships, evaporates fluids, and fulfils besides, I know not how many other purposes. Man, from his infirmity, makes a special tool for every special purpose. God uses one thing for many purposes. Man has often tried to make an instrument which will perfectly serve several different ends, and never entirely succeeded. In God's work, on the other hand, we constantly see many ends met, and met perfectly, by one and the same most simple arrangement.

The consequence of this is, that the difference is immense between looking upon God's work and looking into it. Merely to look upon His work in nature, shews, indeed, that the hand that made it is divine. The first glance, cursory as it may be, gives a satisfying impression, an impression of perfectness. But how much lies beyond this superficial glance! We look out on nature in any form—hills, dales, woods, rocks, trees, water; whatever it is we look on round us, the first glance is enough to give us the impression of perfectness. But in each part of that scene, so cursorily glanced at, every minutest portion will bear the strictest inspection, for every minutest part is perfect. Each blade of grass in all that wide-spread landscape, each worthless, perishing blade of grass, will bear the closest scrutiny; for it is finished by a master's hand. Look at the humblest plant; consider its wondrous mechanism; its vessels for imbibing nourishment from the earth, and nourishment from the air and light; its perfect and complete apparatus for preserving and increasing its allotted growth. Look at the vilest and most insignificant insect that creeps up that unthought-of stem, whose life is but a fleeting hour; for that hour finding all its wants supplied, and its powers, one and all, adapted and perfect to their appointed end. Think of these things, and then we shall be better able to enter somewhat into the perfectness of the work of God.

And God's Word, in all these particulars, is like God's work; yea, God's Word is His work as much as creation; and it is its infinite depth and breadth, and the diverse and manifold ends and aims of all we find in it, which make it what it is, inexhaustible. To look, therefore, on the mere surface of the Bible, is one thing; to look into it quite another; for each part may have many purposes. The very words which, in one dispensation and to one people, conveyed a literal command, to be obeyed literally, may, in another age and dispensation, supply a type of some part of God's work or purpose; while in the selfsame passage the humble believer of every age may find matter of comfort or warning, according to his need.

The microscope may be used here as well as in the

physical world. And as in nature those wonders which the microscope presents to us, though it may be but in an insect's wing or a drop of water, give us at a glance a sense of the perfectness of God's work, such as we might not receive even from a view of the boundless heavens, testifying with a voice not to be misunderstood, how wondrous is the Hand that formed them, with whom nothing is too insignificant to be perfected: so His Word, in its more neglected portions, in those passages which we have perhaps thought of comparatively little value, shews the same perfectness. The finishing of the emblems in the Types is by the same hand that finished redemption; the one was, if you please, His great work, the other His small one; but both are His work, and both perfect.

And this His work in His Word has another striking resemblance to His work in creation. Just as in creation, one leading idea is presented throughout it, which testifies in everything we look upon, in every leaf, in every insect, in every blade of grass, to the wisdom, power, and goodness of the Creator,—a testimony which the partial and apparent contradictions of tempests and earthquakes does not alter or disannul; so has all Scripture one great thought stamped on it, which it is bringing out on every side continually,—every act, every history shews it,—that thought is the grace of the Redeemer. There is neither speech nor language, but in all we hear the wondrous tale. Christ is throughout the key to Scripture. He is the one great idea of the Bible. Know Christ, understand God's thoughts about

Him, and then you will understand the Bible.   We are in the dark because we know so little of Him.

I have commenced my inquiry into the Typical Offerings with these remarks, because I am disposed to think that there is with many a feeling,—not perhaps openly expressed, though not on that account the less acted on,—that some portions of the Scriptures, such as the Types, are less valuable and less instructive. But whence have we got this notion?   Not from God. Were these typical parts of Scripture unimportant, God would not have given us so many chapters which really contain no meaning for us, except they have a typical import; respecting which He yet testifies that they are profitable to aid and instruct the man of God. "*All Scripture* is given by inspiration, and *is profitable;*" and this not to mere babes in Christ, but to the man of God,—"that *the man of God* may be perfect, thoroughly furnished to all good works." *

The Types are, in fact, a set of pictures or emblems, directly from the hand of God, by which He would teach His children things otherwise all but incomprehensible.   In the Types, if I may be allowed the expression, God takes His Son to pieces.   By them does He bring within the range of our capacity definite views of the details of Christ's work, which perhaps but for these pictures we should never fully, or at least so fully, apprehend.   The realities which the Types represent are in themselves truths and facts the most elevated, facts which have taken place before God

* 2 Tim. iii. 16, 17.

Himself, facts in which He has Himself been the actor. These vast and infinite objects He brings close before us in emblems, and presents them to our eyes in a series of pictures, with the accuracy of One who views these things as they are seen and understood by Himself, and in a way in which they may be seen and understood by us.

The real secret of the neglect of the Types, I cannot but think may in part be traced to this,—that they require more spiritual intelligence than many Christians can bring to them. To apprehend them requires a certain measure of spiritual capacity and habitual exercise in the things of God, which all do not possess, for want of abiding fellowship with Jesus. The mere superficial glance upon the Word in these parts brings no corresponding idea to the mind of the reader. The types are, indeed, pictures, but to understand the picture it is necessary we should know something of the reality. The most perfect representation of a steam-engine to a South-sea savage would be wholly and hopelessly unintelligible to him, simply because the reality, the outline of which was presented to him, was something hitherto unknown. But let the same drawing be shewn to those who have seen the reality, such will have no difficulty in explaining the representation. And the greater the acquaintance with the reality, the greater will be the ability to explain the picture. The savage who had never seen the steam-engine would of course know nothing whatever about it. Those who had seen an engine but know nothing of its principles, though they might tell the general object of the drawing, could not explain the details. But the engineer, to whom every screw and bolt are familiar, to whom the use and object of each part is thoroughly known, would not only point out where each of these was to be found in the picture, but would shew, what others might overlook, how in different engines these might be made to differ.

It is just so in the Types. He who knows much of the reality will surely also know something of the type. The real secret of our difficulty is that we know so little, and, what is worse, we do not know our ignorance. And the natural pride of our hearts, which does not like to confess our ignorance, or to go through the deep searchings of soul which attend learning and abiding in God's presence, excuses itself under the plea that these things are not important, or, at least, nonessential. Paul had to meet the same spirit in several of the early churches. Thus, in his Epistle to the Hebrews, when about to prove from a type the doctrine of Christ's everlasting priesthood, he speaks of Him as " a priest for ever after the order of Melchisedec," he cannot go on with the proof without telling the Hebrews how much of the difficulty of the subject was to be traced not so much to its own abstruseness as to their spiritual childhood and ignorance. " Of whom," says he, speaking of Melchisedec, " I have many things to say, and hard to be uttered, seeing ye are dull of hearing. For when for the time ye ought to be teachers, ye have need that one teach you which be the first

principles of the oracles of God; and are become such as
have need of milk, and not of strong meat." *   It was
their infancy in Christ, their lack of growth, which hindered their understanding the Scriptures.   As in the
natural world life and intelligence are different, just so
is it in the spiritual.   A man may be born of God, and
as such, having the life of Christ, be an heir of heaven,
sure of all that the love of God has laid up in store for
the redeemed family in glory ; and yet, like a child,
know nothing of his inheritance, nothing of his Father's
will, be a stranger to service and warfare, and ready to
be deceived by any.

This is, I fear, the case with many believers now.
The low standard of truth in the Church, making the
possession of eternal life the end instead of the beginning of the Christian's course, has led many to think
that if they have, or can at last obtain, this life, it is
enough.   But these are not God's thoughts.   Birth,
spiritual birth, is birth of God for ever,—a life once
given never to be destroyed.   Schooling, training,
adorning, clothing, follow the possession of life, and
even the knowledge of it.   I own, indeed, that while
the Christian is a babe, he needs milk, and ought never
to be pressed to service : at such a time he does not
need the deeper truths of Scripture ; strong meat may
choke the babe as much as poison.   But milk, the
simpler doctrines of the Word, will not support the
man in active service.   The man of God needs deeper
truth : and it is, I believe, the lack of this deeper truth

* Heb. v. 12, 13.   See also 1 Cor. iii. 1, 2.

in the Church which so effectually leaves us without power or service, and brings it to pass that much of what is done is performed in the energy of the flesh rather than in the power of the Spirit.

I must add one word in connexion with the passage just alluded to, which, though beside our present object, may not really be beside the mark. It is written, "Strong meat belongeth to them that are of full age, even those who by reason of use have their senses exercised to discern both good and evil." * It is "*by reason of use*," that is, by using the truth we already possess, that the senses are exercised to advance further. Let us act up faithfully to the light we have, use out fully the grace already given, then surely our spiritual strength will not only rapidly but wonderfully increase.

But it is time I should turn particularly to the object more immediately before us,—*The Types in general; their characteristic differences in the different books of the Old Testament.*

It is pretty generally known that in the Old Testament there are typical persons, things, times, and actions; but it is not, I believe, so generally known how remarkably these types vary in character, and how beautifully they have been divided and arranged by God himself under different classes, if I may so speak; each one distinct from the others, and each having something characteristic. The books of the Old Testament are God's divisions; each of them may be called one of God's chapters; and in each of these books we find

* Heb. v. 14.

something different as respects the character of **the** Types they contain. The general notion of the Types is that they are merely sketches. This is very far short of the truth. So far from being rough sketches, they are one and all most perfectly finished with a master's hand : and a tolerable acquaintance with the distinct character of the different books, and of their types, is enough at once to prove this. Christ is indeed the key to them all : He is the key of the Types, and the key to the Bible. Of Him God has given us more than sketches ; the Word from end to end is full of Him. In the Word we have a whole Christ presented to us : Christ in His offices ; in His character ; in His person ; Christ in His relations to God and man ; Christ in His body the Church ; Christ as giving to God all that God required from man ; Christ as bringing to man all that man required from God ; Christ as seen in this dispensation in suffering ; Christ as seen in the next dispensation in glory ; Christ as the first and the last ; as "all and in all" to His people. The different books are but God's chapters in which He arranges and illustrates some one or more of these or other aspects of His Beloved.

Many are satisfied to see nothing of this : the sprinkled blood in Egypt is enough for them. And this, indeed, secures salvation : but, oh ! how much lies beyond ! Knowing only the blood in Egypt will never teach us our priestly office, nor the value and use of the offerings of the Lord, nor the will of the Lord respecting us. The blood, indeed, wherever seen, bespeaks our safety, and it is blessed even in Egypt to know God's claim is met; but ought we not also, as His redeemed and loved ones, to desire to know more also of His will and our portion?

We know but little of all this as yet, but we know enough to make us long for more. As an old writer has well said, contrasting the dispensations, God in the Types of the last dispensation was teaching His children their letters. In this dispensation He is teaching them to put these letters together, and they find that the letters, arrange them as we will, spell Christ, and nothing but Christ. In the next dispensation He will teach us what Christ means. This is most true. But the Church "as now risen with Christ," as already "seated in heavenly places," * and "in the kingdom," ought even now in spirit to enter a little more into the truth of what Christ has been for us and to us. The Lord teach us all more of His infinite fulness.

I said there was a distinct difference in the Types of the Old Testament, and that this difference is apparently so arranged on purpose, the different classes of types for the most part being found in different books. For my own part I cannot doubt the fact, though I feel it will be quite another thing for me to commend it to others. Take, however, first my statement, and then I will endeavour, in dependence on the Lord, to give the proof which may be brought in support of it.

Those who are so far acquainted with the earlier books of the Bible as to be able to carry their general

* Eph. ii. 6.

contents in their memories, will at once recollect how very different in character some of these books are from others ; some, as for example Genesis, being throughout simple narratives ; others, like Leviticus, being from first to last a series of ceremonial observances.   Each of these books,—those which deal in narrative, as much as those which contain emblematical ordinances,—are, as we find from the New Testament, typical.   There is, however, a great difference in the character of their types ; and to this distinction I now direct attention.

Generally speaking the difference is this.   The types of Genesis foreshadow *God's great dispensational purposes respecting man's development ;* shewing in mystery His secret will and way respecting the different successive dispensations.   The types of Exodus—I speak, of course, generally—bring out, as their characteristic, *redemption and its consequences ;* a chosen people are here redeemed out of bondage, and brought into a place of nearness to God.   Leviticus again differs from each of these, dealing, I think I may say solely, in types connected with *access to God.*   Numbers and Joshua are again perfectly different, the one giving us types connected with *our pilgrimage as in the wilderness ;* the other, types of *our place as over Jordan,* that is, as dead and risen with Christ.   In speaking thus, I would by no means be understood to say that Genesis is the only book which contains dispensational types : I believe that there are many in the other books ; but, wherever this is the case, the dispensational type is subservient to, or rather in connexion with, the special subject of

THE TYPES IN GENERAL.

the book. Thus, if Numbers is the book of the wilderness, the dispensational types in it, if there are any, will bear on the wilderness.*

Nor are these the only books of the Old Testament in which a characteristic and typical thought may be easily traced. I feel satisfied that had we but sufficient intelligence, the remaining books might be viewed in the same manner.† But I take the opening ones as being generally more familiar to us, and sufficient to shew my meaning.

But it may be asked, what proof is there for these assertions? I answer, the New Testament itself seems to me to supply the proof in every case. Of course, as in every other study, a certain amount of apprehension is needed in those to whom the proof is submitted. All have not intelligence enough to grasp the proofs of astronomy, which, nevertheless, are proofs and unanswerable proofs to those whose senses are sufficiently exercised to discern them. So, I doubt not, will it be here. And I venture to say that those who know most of spiritual communion,—who, in God's presence, have entered the deepest into the value of Christ and God's thoughts about Him,—these will be the persons best qualified rightly to estimate the amount of proof contained in what I now suggest to them.

* The history in the thirty-second chapter, I believe, supplies an instance.

† The history recorded in the books of Kings and Chronicles is a good illustration of this. The same persons come before us in both, but with a different object in each. The typical character of the respective books will supply the key to the points of difference.

To return, then, to GENESIS. I said that its types, for the most part, were of a dispensational character, *shewing God's great dispensational purposes,* and the course appointed for man's development. Perhaps it may be necessary for me to explain what I mean by "dispensational purposes." God has, since the fall of man, at various periods dealt with man, in different degrees of intimacy, and, in a certain sense, also on different principles. Throughout all, He has had one purpose in view, to reveal what He is, and to shew what man is; but this one end has been brought out in different ways, and under various and repeated trials.

The sum is this. Man by disobedience fell, and thenceforth has, with all his progeny, been a sinner. The different dispensations, while, on the one hand, they were revelations of God, were also the trial whether, under any circumstances, man could recover himself. God first tried man without law; the end of that was the flood, "for the earth was filled with violence." * God then committed power to Noah, trying man under the restraints of human authority,— saying, "He that sheddeth man's blood, by man shall his blood be shed," † to see, if I may so speak, whether, with this help, man could in any measure recover himself. The end of that, and this within no long period, was open and wide-spread idolatry. God himself then came more manifestly forth as a giver. The other dispensations are specially His. He chose one family,—

* Gen. vi. 11.   † Gen. ix. 6.

the family of Abraham,—and, to give man in the flesh every assistance in recovering himself, He gave him a perfect law, to see whether by this law he could improve or restore himself. This was the dispensation of the law. I need not tell you the end of this. God sent His servants seeking fruit of the husbandmen to whom He had let out His vineyard; and some they beat, and some they stoned, and all they treated shamefully. Last of all He sent His Son, and Him they cast out and crucified.* Such was the end of this first dispensation, and of the experiment whether man in the flesh could be amended by law. God then brought in a new thing, the dispensation of resurrection,—I mean the Christian dispensation,—differing from the preceding in this point, above all others, that it did not recognize man in the flesh at all, but only owned, as the subjects of a heavenly kingdom, such as were quickened by a new and heavenly life. Man in the flesh was now no more to be tried, for it was a settled thing that he was utterly lost and helpless,—and baptism sealed this.† God would now Himself make a people,

* Matt. xxi. 33–39.

† The contrast between baptism and circumcision is most characteristic of their respective dispensations. Circumcision, as we are told in Peter, (chap. iii. 21.) represented " *the putting away the filth of the flesh.*" This was all the old dispensation aimed at; for it assumed that the flesh could be improved. Man, therefore, the seed of Abraham according to the flesh, was in the flesh taken into covenant. Baptism, on the contrary, as we are repeatedly told, (Rom. vi.; Col. ii.; 1 Pet. iii.) represents *the death and burial of the flesh:* for this dispensation starts on the ground that the flesh is incurable, and that it is only as quickened by the Spirit that man can come to

"begotten again by the resurrection of Christ,"* who
through this dispensation of grace should be a witness,
not of what they were, but of what He was. A dispensation, therefore, was begun, not owning man in the
flesh in any way, in which God has been dealing almost
in direct contrast to His dealings with man under the
law. This is the present dispensation.

I have perhaps enlarged on this question more than
my subject demands, but the importance of it may be
my apology,—an importance, I grieve to say, but little
recognized by the mass of Christians. What I have
said, however, will shew how God has dealt with man
dispensationally,—that is, how, in different ages and
dispensations, His requirements and laws have varied.
God's first dispensation was the law: His second is
the gospel.

Now the types of Genesis, unlike those of some of
the other books, are taken up, I may say almost exclusively, with foreshadowings of great truths or events
connected with these dispensations. Two or three
passages from the New Testament will supply a
divinely-authorized proof of this statement. With
these, as a starting-point, I trust I shall easily shew
how full Genesis is of similar types.

Let us look, then, for a moment at Gen. xxi., with

God; in a word, that except a man be born again he cannot see the
kingdom of God. And the believer, having this new birth, is called
to profess the worthlessness of the flesh, in an ordinance which, if
rightly administered, is as strikingly representative of the design of
this, as circumcision was of the design of the old covenant.

* 1 Pet. i. 3.

St Paul's comment on it in Gal. iv.:—"Tell me, ye that desire to be under the law, do ye not hear the law? For it is written, that Abraham had two sons; the one by a bond-maid, the other by a free-woman. But he who was of the bond-woman was born after the flesh; but he of the free-woman was by promise. Which things are an allegory: for these are the two covenants; the one from the mount Sinai, which gendereth to bondage, which is Agar. For this Agar is mount Sinai in Arabia, and answereth to Jerusalem which now is, and is in bondage with her children. But Jerusalem which is above is free, which is the mother of us all. . . . . But as then he that was born after the flesh persecuted him that was born after the Spirit, even so it is now. Nevertheless what saith the Scripture? Cast out the bond-woman and her son: for the son of the bond-woman shall not be heir with the son of the free-woman."*

Now all this is *dispensational*. Hagar, the hand-maid, and a bond-woman, stands the perfect type of the covenant of law: Sarah, the true wife, and a free-woman, the representative of the covenant of grace. The first son, Ishmael, born according to nature, a type of the Jew, who by natural birth came into covenant. The second son, Isaac, born contrary to nature, of parents who were " as good as dead," † a type of the resurrection life of this dispensation, the life from above springing out of death. I can but just touch the subject here; but enough perhaps has been said to shew my

* Gal. iv. 21–81. † Heb. xi. 12; Rom. iv. 19.

B

meaning. Christ, of course, is the key here as elsewhere; yet how different here from the types of Leviticus, which, instead of speaking of Him as connected
with dispensations, shew His work as bearing on communion. And if the types of Genesis are unlike Leviticus, what shall we say of Numbers and Joshua,
which in their types are full, as we shall see, of representations of the varied experience of the redeemed?
The least measure of spiritual intelligence must, I
think, at once apprehend a difference so striking as this.

I cannot leave the type of Hagar and Sarah without
just noticing one other part in it, which may not be
altogether thrown away. Observe, when Sarah died,
Abraham took again another wife, Keturah;* and by
her he had, not one son, as in the preceding types, (one
son in each being the emblem of one family,) but
many sons, the type of that which shall take place
when the Sarah dispensation is ended: when not one
nation only shall be the Lord's, but when "the king-
doms of this world" shall be His. Hitherto God has
had but one nation: in the last dispensation a peculiar
nation in the flesh; now a peculiar nation in the
spirit, whose birth is not from Adam, but from
Christ. But in the next dispensation it will be
otherwise. The Sarah covenant will never embrace
the nations, though it will "take out of them a people
for His name," † for in it "there is neither Jew nor
Greek;" the flesh, as I have said, in it being in no way
recognized. It will be otherwise when the next dispen-

* Gen. xxv. 1-4.   † Acts xv. 14.

sation comes, and "the earth is filled with the knowledge of the Lord." But I am to speak of the characteristic difference of the Types, and not of all that is taught us in them.

A second passage from the book of Genesis, which is referred to in the New Testament as typical, is the history of Melchisedec. In the seventh of Hebrews the apostle is shewing the abrogation and disannulling of the Levitical priesthood, and how the dispensation of the law, with the things pertaining to it, was superseded by a new dispensation. In support of this, he refers to a fact recorded in Genesis, which he uses as his sufficient proof. The passage is very remarkable, not only as shewing the character of the types of Genesis, but as teaching us something of the nature of typical representations, and of the way in which they must be interpreted. But I here simply refer to it as an instance in point, to shew the general character of the types of Genesis. The history tells us that Abraham paid tithes to Melchisedec, one who in his own person was both king and priest. The apostle shews how every detail given of this person, yea, and how that also which is omitted respecting him, is all full of typical instruction.* Levi paid tithes in Abraham to

* I refer here to the fact noticed by the apostle, that in Melchisedec's history there is no record either of his birth or death,—an omission very unusual in Scripture with those who take a prominent place; which omission, however, the apostle shews to be typical. Melchisedec, says Paul, was "without father or mother, without descent, having neither beginning of days, nor end of life." He does not mean that Melchisedec really had none of these; but that

Melchisedec: that proves, says the apostle, how far Levi was below Melchisedec. It speaks, also, of a time when the priesthood of Levi will have to yield to another priesthood. I do not go into details: they are sufficiently familiar to those even moderately versed in Scripture. I only refer to it as another undoubted illustration of the *dispensational character* of the types of Genesis.

Take another of the types of Genesis,—I mean the history of Joseph. No one, I suppose, who has ever thought upon it, can doubt that this history is typical. But typical of what? Of *dispensational truth.* Joseph is the eldest son of the younger and best-loved wife. Here, again, we get the two wives, as in a former instance, bringing out the same truth, though with some additions. Leah, the elder wife, has all her children before Rachel, the younger, has any. The Jewish dispensation had all its children before the Christian dispensation had any. Christ, the first-born from the grave, was the first son of the Rachel dispensation. This son, the beloved of his father, is cast out by his brethren, the children of the elder wife, and cast into Egypt, the constant type of the Gentile world. There, after a season of suffering and shame, he is exalted to be head over the kingdom; his wife is given him from out of the Gentiles, and then his brethren, the children of the first wife, know him. This type, I think, needs

none are recorded in his history, and that this omission is distinctly typical. We shall find, as we proceed, that the omissions in the types of Leviticus are as full of import as the facts recorded.

no explanation: if explanation be needed, the eleventh of
Romans will supply it. The sin of the Jews, the elder
brethren, is made the riches of the Gentiles for a season,
until the elder brethren in need are brought to know
and worship their brother, and are reconciled to Him.
But I wish merely to call attention to the fact, that
here, as elsewhere in Genesis, the types are *dispensational.* Christ rejected by the Jewish family, and His
history among the Gentiles, and again the restoration
of His brethren to Him: this is the history of Joseph.

I will give but one more example, which must suffice
for my proof as to the book of Genesis. Take, then, the
ark of Noah. If there be a type in the Bible, the ark is
surely a type,—of Christ without doubt,—but of Christ
viewed *dispensationally.* Indeed, St Peter expressly
refers to it in this light, as a type of the mystical
death and resurrection of the Church in Christ.* But
to look at the history. We have first an old world to
be destroyed, with one faithful family upon it, or rather
one family who are saved for the faithfulness and piety
of their head, as it is said,—" Come thou, and all thy
house, into the ark: for thee have I seen righteous."†
Then we have a new world coming forth in beauty,
after destruction has passed on the old; while the
chosen family are brought from the one world to the
other, in an ark, the only place of safety. Christ is
the Ark, taking the chosen family from the world of
judgment to the new heavens and the new earth. This

* 1 Pet. iii. 21, ᾧ ἀντίτυπον, κ. τ. λ.
† Gen. vii. 1.

is clear; but look at the details. May I not say, the microscope may be used here? The ark, with all its burden, rests on the mountains of the new world, months before any portion of that new world could be seen. Christ, as our Ark, has rested in resurrection, with all the redeemed family in Him; for in Him we are already "risen," while as yet the waters of judgment (for "now is the judgment of this world,"*) are resting on the world. And mark the foreknowledge of God; the day the ark rested was the very day and the very month on which, ages afterwards, Christ, the true Ark, rested in resurrection. "The ark rested on the seventh month, on the seventeenth day of the month." † On that day Christ rose from the dead. The fourteenth day of this seventh month (afterwards, by God's command, called the first month, ‡) was the passover; the fifteenth, the feast of unleavened bread; § and the third day from that, "the seventeenth day," was the day Christ rose from the dead.

But I have said enough to shew the character of the types of Genesis, and that they are all more or less *dispensational*. And let it be observed we have in them three dispensations,—the past, the present, and a future one.

I now pass on more briefly to speak of the general character of the types of EXODUS. These, as I have already said, are chiefly connected with *redemption*

---

* John xii. 31.   † Gen. viii. 4.   ‡ Exod. xii. 2.
§ Lev. xxiii. 5, 6; compare this with Matt. xxvi. 17; Luke xxii. 7; and John xviii. 28.

and its consequences. In proof of this, as in the former case, I will begin with New Testament evidence.

Let us, then, begin with the Passover, the institution of which is recorded in the twelfth chapter. Is there a doubt on the mind of any whether or not this ordinance is to be regarded as typical? Then let us hear Paul's comment upon it: "Christ our passover is sacrificed for us: therefore let us keep the feast, not with the old leaven, neither with the leaven of malice and wickedness; but with the unleavened bread of sincerity and truth."* And what is this passover but *redemption*? The elect family, with shoes on their feet, and their loins girt ready for flight from Egypt, are standing by night ("the night is far spent"†) within the house whose door-posts are sprinkled with blood, while the destroying angel is abroad in judgment, in the death of their first-born judging the pride of Egypt.

And this is the one great truth in Egypt,—the sprinkled blood, and its value as delivering from judgment. In Egypt it is much to know that Israel is redeemed, and that there is safety in the blood of sprinkling. But the blood of Jesus has much more connected with it than mere deliverance from Egypt or salvation; yet this is the only use of it which is known by Israel in the house of bondage. For Israel in Egypt, for the Christian in the world, the one great truth is the Passover, redemption through the blood of the Lamb, salvation, not for our righteousness' sake, but because the blood is on the door-post. To learn

* 1 Cor. v. 7, 8. † Rom. xiii. 12.

anything further of the uses of that blood, Israel must
be brought to know themselves out of Egypt, to see
themselves as the redeemed of the Lord, and that God
doth put a difference between them and the Egyptians.
It is in the wilderness, in separation from Egypt, that
God opens to His people all the value of the Offerings.
There is no knowledge of the burnt-offering in Egypt,
or of its difference from the meat-offering or the sin-
offering; there is no knowledge of the laver or shew-
bread there, or of the blessed work which the priest
performs. All this is learnt when Israel is in truth a
pilgrim, with the Red Sea and Egypt behind him.

How true is all this in our experience. Look at saints
who do not fully know redemption; what is the only
truth for them? Just this—the passover, the sprinkled
blood; they have no heart or eyes to see any further.
But I am again going into the type, rather than point-
ing out its general bearing, *redemption*.

And that this is the general character of the types
of Exodus, will, I think, be apparent to such as
endeavour, in dependence on the Lord, to read the
book as a whole, and to grasp the one great thought
which throughout is stamped on it. What is the
exodus from Egypt but redemption? What is the
march through the sea but redemption? This is the
key-note of Israel's song when Pharaoh and his hosts
are fallen :—" Thou in Thy mercy, O Lord, hast led
forth Thy people which *Thou hast redeemed:* . . .
fear shall fall on the inhabitants of Canaan, till the
people pass over, whom *Thou hast purchased.* Thou

shalt bring them in."* And in keeping with this commencement, the types in the latter part of the book are occupied with representations of the consequences of redemption,—a people brought near to God.

LEVITICUS differs from all this. That it is typical, I need hardly say: for unless we look at it as such, it has—I say it with reverence—for us no meaning. But the Epistles of the New Testament are full of direct references, which prove beyond a doubt the typical character of its ordinances.† Of these references, there are not less than forty, every one of which speaks of the things referred to as typical. But typical of what? Of Christ, clearly. But of Christ under what aspect? Not as *connected with dispensations,* as we see Him in the types of Genesis; not as *teaching redemption,* as we see Him in the earlier types of Exodus. Leviticus begins after redemption is known, and speaks of things *connected with the access of a chosen people to God.* Thus, as the following pages I trust will shew, though Christ in His work is the sum and substance of these types, it is Christ as discerned by one who already knows the certainty of redemption : it is Christ as seen by one, who, possessing peace with God and deliverance, is able to look with joy at all that Christ has so fully been for him. Christ as the priest, the offerer, the offering; Christ as meeting all that a saved sinner needs to approach to God ; Christ for the believer, and all that Christ is to the believer, as keeping up his

* Exod. xv. 13, 16, 17.
† Heb. v. vii. viii. ix. x. xiii. I Pet. ii. &c. &c.

communion with God; this is what we have distinctly
set forth in the varied types of Leviticus. Exodus
gives us the blood of the lamb, saving Israel in the
land of Egypt. Leviticus gives us the priest and the
offerings, meeting Israel's need in *their access to
Jehovah.*

But I do not enter into details here, as the Offerings
will supply a sufficient proof. I pass on therefore to
the types of Numbers, to mark what appears to me to
be their distinctive character.

NUMBERS, — giving the history of Israel in the
wilderness, their services, their trials, and their failures
there,—brings out, I cannot doubt, repeated types of
the *Christian's experience and pilgrimage in the
world as in a wilderness.* Israel's history, as well as
Israel's ordinances, was typical; their coming out of
Egypt was typical; their sojourn in the wilderness was
typical; their entering the land was typical; and the
details of each of these portions of their history, the
typical character of which in general is granted by all,
will shew how perfectly the pictures are finished by
the hand of One who well knew what He was
describing.

In Numbers, then, we get types connected with the
wilderness. Here the world is viewed not as the house
of bondage, but as the place of trial, the scene of
pilgrimage, through which Israel must pass to Canaan.*

---

* In Exodus we get just the reverse, the world viewed, not as our
place of pilgrimage, but as the kingdom of Pharaoh and the house
of bondage.

Thus, in those chapters in Numbers which are most allied in their character to the types of Leviticus, (where the offering of Christ, as in "the red heifer," is without doubt the great end of the representation,*) we have the sacrifice, not as in Leviticus, shewing some aspect of Christ's offering as bearing on communion, but as further coming in with particular application to the trials of a walk of faith in the wilderness; and meeting the cases of individual experience, such as contact with evil, or any other defilement.

I speak the less on this subject, because the whole character of the book is so obvious,† and to enter into the particulars would fill a volume. Suffice it to say, throughout we have the elect in the wilderness, learning there what man is, and what God is; what the ransomed people ought to be, and what they really are. We have the Levites,—I take one undoubted type from the fourth chapter,—the picture of the Church in service, with garments unspotted from pollution, passing onwards through the desert land; each day dependent on God for everything, and following the guidance of the fire and cloud, while they bear the vessels of the sanctuary, and care for them in the dreary waste. Those vessels all typified something of

* Numbers xix. The red heifer was the only sin-offering in which the fat of the inwards was not burnt on the altar. But this is in exact keeping with the character of the book of Numbers, giving us the offering only in its relation to the wilderness. The fat on the altar would have been God's part. In Numbers, therefore, this is unnoticed.

† See St Paul's application of the history in 1 Cor x. 1-11.

Christ. And the spiritual Levites have now to bear
Him through the wilderness.

And so throughout, Numbers gives us *the wilderness.*
The pillar of cloud preceding them;* the blowing of
the silver trumpets, and the alarm in the camp;† the
murmuring after the flesh-pots of Egypt;‡ and the
shrinking through unbelief from going up to Canaan;§
—fit representation of God's chosen people shrinking
backward from the trials of their heavenly calling;—
the want of water in the wilderness, and the stony rock
opened to supply that need;‖ the whoredom with the
daughters of Moab,¶ and the discouragement because
of the way;** what are all these but living pictures of
the Christian pilgrim's experience *as in the wilderness?*

How different is JOSHUA from all this; experience
again, I doubt not, but what different experience. The
one teaching us our way in the wilderness, the other as
already beyond Jordan in the land. Into this I fear
some may find it more difficult to enter, because the
reality which is represented is a thing unknown to
them. Joshua teaches us, in type, *the Church already
with Christ in heavenly places,* and but few saints apprehend this experience, or know what resurrection
means. Thus the book of Joshua, if viewed typically,
answers very nearly to the Epistle to the Ephesians.
In either book we see the elect standing in the place of

* Chapter ix.   † Chapter x.   ‡ Chapter xi.
§ Chapters xiii. xiv.   ‖ Chapter xx.
¶ Chapter xxiii.   ** Chapter xxi.

promise, but finding it still a place of conflict. As
Paul says, " We are raised up, and made to sit together
in heavenly places in Christ:"* but that place is
not yet the rest; for, as he proceeds in the same
Epistle, " We wrestle not against flesh and blood,
but against principalities and powers *in heavenly
places.*"†

The book of Joshua is just this. It describes to us
Israel passing from the wilderness over Jordan into the
land of Canaan. All these are emblems familiar to us.
Jordan, as we all know, is the type of death, dividing
the wilderness, this world, from the land of promise,
heaven. Israel passes through Jordan without feeling
its waters, and comes with Joshua into the promised
land. When he passes Jordan, all Israel passes. And
thus it was in Christ. The Church is dead with Him,
buried with Him, risen with Him; but there is still a
conflict, for the Canaanite will dwell in that land.
And so it will be till the true Solomon comes. Oh, may
He hasten His coming!

But let us take an example or two as illustrating
this. In the fourth chapter we read of Israel crossing
Jordan dryshod: in the fifth we read of their circumcision. As soon as they are over Jordan, so soon are
they all called to be circumcised. Though the seed of
Abraham, there had been no circumcision for Israel in
the wilderness; but as soon as they come into the land,
circumcision begins at once. Need I explain what this

* Eph. ii. 6.
† Eph. vi. 12, *ἐν τοῖς ἐπουρανίοις*, the same as in ch. i. 6.

is, or shew how exactly it answers to "the eighth day" of the original institution? Circumcision was to be "*on the eighth day*."* To those at all familiar with the types, I need not say that "the eighth day" is always typical of resurrection. The eighth day, the day after the seventh or Sabbath, answers to "the first day of the week" on which Christ rose: it is however "the first day" in reference to seven having gone before. Seven days include the periods proper to the first creation. The eighth day, as it takes us beyond and out of these,—that is, beyond the limits of the old creation,—brings us in type into a new order of things and times, in a word, into the new creation or resurrection. With regard to circumcision, we are taught in Peter, that it represented "the putting away the filth of the flesh." To do this was the great attempt of the whole Jewish dispensation, and that attempt ended in failure; for resurrection, the place beyond Jordan, was not yet occupied by Israel. But since Christ, the true Joshua, has passed through Jordan, and since all the Church is in and with Him,—and because, as members of His body, the Church is dead and risen with Him,— *therefore* it is called to be circumcised, and to put away the filth of the flesh. "*If ye be risen* with Christ . . . *put off anger, wrath, malice, blasphemy.*"† True circumcision of the heart is only known and attained to in proportion as we know the power of the resurrection.

But to speak of other parts; how different through-

---

* Gen. xvii. 8; Phil. iii. 5.   † Col. iii. 1, 3, 5, 8.

out is the experience of the books of Numbers and Joshua. Not that in fact the two can really be separated, for in Christ the Church is apprehended for everything : but it is one thing to be apprehended of Him, and another to apprehend that for which we are apprehended.* One portion of experience is often more apprehended than another. Indeed, our experience is but the measure of our individual attainment, the extent to which we have proved the truth, the apprehension in our own souls of that which is already true for us in Christ. The work of Christ for us has brought His members into every blessing, and faith at once rests on this; but experience only apprehends that amount of this which is realized in our souls by the Holy Ghost.

But to return to the difference of Numbers and Joshua. There was no difficulty in possessing the wilderness ; but Israel had to fight for every step in the land. Instead of lusting for flesh as in the wilderness, in the land, in the knowledge of resurrection, the temptation is quite of another sort. We have confidence in strength, as before Ai ;† confidence in knowledge, as in the case of the Gibeonites ;‡ abusing grace, as in the case of Achan ; understanding how it gives victory, but not seeing God's claims in it. As saints grow in grace and in the knowledge of their place as even now risen, they have another class of trials to meet in addition to the trials of the wilderness, " the wrestling, not with flesh and blood, but with

* Phil. iii. 12. † Chapter vii. ‡ Chapter ix.

principalities and powers in heavenly places." **And** this is in fact the book of Joshua.

Such is a very brief and imperfect sketch of the different character of some of the typical parts of Scripture. I feel how little what I have said will convey to one who has not studied it, the exceeding depth and fulness of my subject.

Does any one say that these are but points of knowledge, and as such of comparatively little value? I grant that they are points of knowledge, but I answer, we grow in grace through knowledge.* And one reason of the weakness of the Church is the shallowness of her knowledge on these points. To shew the use of this knowledge is not my present purpose. Suffice it to say, that were the types of Genesis understood, we should not see such grievous mistakes arising from confounding the dispensations, and mingling the things and hopes of one covenant with the things and hopes of another. And so of the rest. Know more of Exodus, that is, of redemption; know more of Leviticus, that is, of the ground of access to God; know more of Numbers, the experience of the wilderness; and of Joshua, the experience as even now beyond Jordan; and then see if you have not something more to use in service for Him who redeemed and loved you.

That thus it may be with us indeed, let us pray that the Lord will keep us near to Himself, in abiding communion with Him. Amen.

* 2 Pet. i. 2.

THE BURNT-OFFERING.

LEVITICUS I.

IN the preceding pages, I have endeavoured to point out the distinctive character of the types in some of the earlier books of the Old Testament. We are now in a better position to estimate the distinctions in the types of this book, Leviticus.

Speaking generally, the types of Leviticus, as I have said, give us *the work of Christ, in its bearing on worship and communion.* We have not here, as in the earlier part of Exodus, the sprinkled blood to redeem from Egypt; but we get definite instruction respecting the Offering and Priest, to meet the need of a saved people in their approaches to God their Saviour. In a word, instead of seeing Christ as redeeming, we here see His work for the redeemed; His work, not in bringing them out of Egypt, but in bringing them into the place of worship, in keeping them there in happy fellowship, and in restoring them when they fail or fall.

And how varied are the aspects of Christ's work, viewed merely in this one relation. To hold communion with God, the redeemed need Christ as *the Offering*; and this is the first view we get of Him in

C

Leviticus: but they need Him also as *the Priest* and Mediator; and therefore this is also another aspect in which He is presented to us. And so we might go on step by step in the consideration of the blessed work of Jesus, passing from one part to another of His service in keeping up and restoring the communion of His redeemed.

The work of Christ, then, as connected with the communion of His people, may, and indeed, if fully apprehended, must be viewed under many different representations. The *offering* is the first representation; the *priest*, in close connexion with it, the second; because it is under these two great aspects that the redeemed in communion with God have most to do with Jesus. At present I purpose going no further than *Christ viewed as the Offering.* Christ as the key to the dispensations, as we see Him in the types of Genesis; — Christ as the ground of redemption, as shewn in the book of Exodus;—Christ the rearer of the tabernacle, and the substance of its many services; —Christ the guide of His people, whether through the wilderness or into the land over Jordan;—Christ as the rejected king while another holds His kingdom;— Christ as the glorious king who builds the temple in Jerusalem:—all these and many other aspects of the work and person of our blessed Lord will, for the present, in some measure be held in abeyance, that we may more particularly enter into this one aspect, this first aspect of Christ, as connected with communion, CHRIST THE SUM OF THE OFFERINGS.

And how much is there to arrest and instruct us in this one simple view of Him. He is the Burnt-offering, the Meat-offering, the Peace-offering, the Sin-offering, and the Trespass-offering for His people.* By His one oblation of Himself once offered, He has stood in all these different relations,—relations so precious to God, that through preceding ages He had the representation of them constantly presented to Him,—relations so needful to the Church, that it is on the apprehension of them that her joy and strength depend. And yet how great a proportion of believers have neither knowledge nor wish to trace these. They read of Him as the Sin-offering and the Burnt-offering; but no corresponding thought is suggested to them by this distinction. It is enough for them that the blood has been sprinkled on the door-post; and they care not to know more of Him who sprinkled it.

But these are not God's thoughts, nor are they the thoughts of those who know the joy of communion with Him. Such go from strength to strength in the knowledge of the grace and work of Jesus. Have they known Him as the paschal lamb in Egypt? they seek then to know Him as the offering within the tabernacle. Have they learnt Him in His different relations as offering? they seek to know Him in all His offices as priest. Do they know Him as priest? they seek Him as prophet, as manna, as water, as guide, as everything. May the Lord only fill us with

* See Heb. x. 4–10.

His Spirit: then we cannot but follow on to know more of Jesus.

But it is time we should turn to THE OFFERINGS.

In approaching them I would make a general observation or two on some particulars which are common to all the Offerings, the right understanding of which may lead us to a clearer apprehension of the principle on which they must be interpreted. Without definite thoughts on each of these particulars, the various types will be little more than unmeaning repetition to us.

(1.) The first point, then, which requires our notice is this:—In each offering there are at least *three distinct objects* presented to us. There is the *offering*, the *priest*, the *offerer*. A definite knowledge of the precise import of each of these is absolutely requisite if we would understand the offerings.

What, then, is *the offering?* what *the priest?* what *the offerer?* Christ is the offering, Christ is the priest, Christ is the offerer. Such and so manifold are the relations in which Christ has stood for man and to man, that no one type or set of types can adequately represent the fulness of them. Thus we have many distinct classes of types, and further variations in these distinct classes, each of which gives us one particular view of Christ, either in His character, or in His work, or person. But see Him as we may for sinners, He fills more than one relation. This causes the necessity of many emblems. First He comes as offerer, but we cannot see the offerer without the offering, and the offerer is Himself the offering, and He who is both offerer and offering is also the priest. As man under the law, our substitute, Christ, stood for us towards God as offerer. He took "the body prepared for Him" as His offering, that in it and by it He might reconcile us to God. Thus, when sacrifice and offering had wholly failed,— when at man's hand God would no more accept them,— " then said He, Lo, I come: in the volume of the book it is written of me, I delight to do Thy will, O God : yea, Thy law is within my heart." * Thus His body was His offering: He willingly offered it; and then as priest He took the blood into the holiest. As *offerer*, we see Him *man under the law*, standing our substitute, for us to fulfil all righteousness. As *priest*, we have Him presented as *the mediator*, God's messenger between Himself and Israel. While as *the offering* He is seen *the innocent victim*, a sweet savour to God, yet bearing the sin and dying for it.

Thus in the selfsame type *the offerer* sets forth Christ *in His person*, as the One who became man to meet God's requirements : *the offering* presents Him *in His character and work*, as the victim by which the atonement was ratified ; while the *priest* gives us a third picture of Him, *in His official relation*, as the appointed mediator and intercessor. Accordingly, when we have a type in which the *offering* is most prominent, the leading thought will be Christ the victim. On the other hand, when the *offerer* or *priest* predominates, it will respectively be Christ as man or Christ as mediator.

Connected with this there is also another particular,

* Heb. x. 5–9; Ps. xl. 6–8.

the import of which must be known to understand **the**
Offerings.   I refer to the laying of the offerer's hands
on the head of the victim offered.   This act *in itself*
was nothing more than the expression of *the identity
of the offerer and offering.*   In each case the giving
up of the offering represented the surrender of the
person of the offerer.   The offering, whatever it might
be, stood for, and was looked upon as identical with
the offerer.   In the one case, in the sweet savour offerings, it represented the offerer as an accepted worshipper, wholly surrendering himself upon the altar of
the Lord, to be a sweet savour to Jehovah.   In the
other case, as in the sin and trespass offerings, where
the offerer came as a sinner with confession, the offerer
in his offering surrendered himself as a sinner to God's
judgment, and was cast out as accursed into the wilderness.   We know Him who stood in both these relations, when in the body prepared for Him " He gave
Himself."

(2.) Another particular to which I would direct
attention respects *the differences between the several
offerings.*   These differences are not a secondary matter.
The very definiteness and distinct character of the particular offerings is wholly involved in them.   Any non-
apprehension, therefore, or misapprehension on this
point, must necessarily leave us in much uncertainty.

As to these differences, then, there are first several
different offerings, as the *Burnt-*offering, the *Meat-*offering, the *Peace-*offering, &c. ; and secondly, there are
different grades of the same offering, as the burnt-

offering *of the herd*, the burnt-offering *of the flock*, the burnt-offering *of fowls;* the peace-offering *of the herd*, the peace-offering *of the flock*, &c. The question is,— or rather it is no question,—have these distinctions any meaning corresponding to them? With regard to all the great outlines in these typical ordinances, every Christian is satisfied that they represent Jesus; yet some doubt whether we are justified in expecting to find Him in every distinct and minute particular. And the fancies which have been vented upon this subject have, indeed, been enough to warn us. Still, my answer to such doubts is simply this,—Are not the particulars, as all Scripture, "written for our learning;" and can they be so if the words are without import, if they are meant to reveal nothing to us? But no. This God's representation of the work of His Beloved will bear looking at as much as His other works. Doubtless here, where every addition is but to depict Christ's fulness, each minutest particular, each variety, has a meaning attached to it. God's words are not here, more than elsewhere, vain words. It is only our want of spiritual apprehension which makes these things so mysterious to us. The shadow may, indeed, be more dark than the substance, but for every shadow there must be a substance; and he that best knows the substance and reality will soonest recognise its darkened shadow. And just as the shadow of this our earth, as it passes over the face of another planet, leads the instructed eye by a glance to the knowledge of facts respecting the form and proportions of the globe we dwell on; so often does the apprehension of one of these shadows which God has marked as cast from the work of Jesus, reveal Him and His work to His people in a way which no less delights than it astonishes them.

The fact is, the true secret respecting the difficulty of the types is, that we are not sufficiently acquainted with the reality; and as a consequence, the representation of that reality is unintelligible or almost unintelligible to us. Only let us see more of Christ; only let us, in God's presence, learn more of Him in all His relations; and then the things which God has thought worthy a place in His Word, because they represent something which may be seen of Jesus, will find an answering place in our intelligence, because they will each find a response in our experience.

But to speak of these *differences*. I have not a doubt that they are intended to represent *different aspects* of Christ's offering. I cannot say how far the proof of this may commend itself to those who are comparatively strangers to such questions, for here as elsewhere a certain measure of previous intelligence is required to enable us rightly to estimate the value of the proof submitted to us. In this field of knowledge too, as in others of a kindred nature, the proof of a fact may be more difficult than the discovery of it; and again, the demonstration of the proof to those unaccustomed to such questions, far more difficult than the demonstration of the fact itself. I doubt not it will be so in this case. I am, however, satisfied as to the fact; I will now endeavour, as briefly as may be, to express what proof may be given of it.

To do this I must again advert to what has already been said respecting the offerer and offering. We have seen that the offerer is Christ, standing as man under the law to fulfil all righteousness. We have seen that the offering represents His body, and the laying on of hands the identity of the offering and offerer. Now in these types we have this offerer and His offering both presented to us in very different circumstances. The faithful Israelite is seen in different aspects, and according to the aspect in which he is regarded, so is his offering dealt with. In one we see him standing as a sinless offerer, offering a sweet-smelling savour for acceptance. In another he stands as a convicted sinner, offering an expiatory sacrifice which bears the penalty of his offences.

Now the offering of Christ, which all these shadows typify, was but one, and but once offered; but the shadows vary in shape and outline according to the point from whence, and the light in which, they are looked upon. In other words, the one offering had several aspects, and each aspect required a separate picture. Had Christ's fulness and relations been less manifold, fewer emblems might have sufficed to represent them; but as they are many, and each to be variously apprehended, no one emblem, however perfect, could depict them all. As priest, or offering, or offerer, He fills a distinct relation, the representation of which necessarily requires a distinct emblem. Yet in each of these relations He may be variously seen, and each of these variations will again require a different picture. Thus as priest He may be seen interceding with God, or sprinkling the leper, or taking in the blood. It is plain that the emblem which might set forth one of these would by no means present another relation of Him. But God's will is that all His relations should be seen; and the consequence is types many and various.

With respect, then, to *the varieties in the offerings*, I conclude that they are but *different aspects* of Christ's work or person. Let us now advance a step further and inquire, What are *the different grades* which we find in the different offerings? Without doubt these proceed on the same principle. They are but different views of this or that peculiar aspect. Not only is Christ's work one which has many aspects, but each aspect may be very differently apprehended, according to the measure of intelligence possessed by those who look at Him. Thus there may be different apprehensions of the same relation, and of the selfsame act in the same relation. For instance, as the offering, one grade of it is the bullock, another the lamb, another the turtle-dove. Now each of these emblems gives us a different thought respecting the value or character of the selfsame offering. One grade shews Christ, and one saint sees Him, as an offering " of the herd," that is the most costly offering. Another gives a lower view of its value, or at least a different view of its character, as in the grade of " the turtle-dove." In every grade, the lowest as much as the highest, the offering is seen to be free from blemish : in every grade it is seen a sufficient offering, meeting all the requirements of the sacrifice ; but the riches of the offerer, and the value and distinct character of his offering, are very differently apprehended in the different pictures.

I conclude, therefore, that as *the different offerings* give us different aspects or relations of Christ's one offering, so *the different grades* in the same offering give us different views or apprehensions of the same aspect.

An illustration may perhaps better express the difference. Suppose, then, several aspects of some building, the north aspect, the south aspect, the west aspect; these would correspond with *the different offerings*, as the burnt-offering, the meat-offering, &c. But there might be three or four views of the building taken from the same side, but under different lights, and at different distances : this would be *the different grades* in the same offering.

And the analogy of the other parts of Scripture directly supports this interpretation; for the different books, as we have seen, looked at typically, do but bring out different aspects or measures of apprehension of that great and perfect work of which all Scripture testifies. One book gives the experience of Egypt; another the experience of the wilderness; another the experience of the land. All these by one act of Jesus are true for the Church in Him; but they are not all equally apprehended; for our experience always comes

far short of the reality, and the reality may be apprehended in very different measures.   Christian experience, as I have before observed, is only our measure
of apprehension of that which is already true for us in
Jesus.   And this measure of apprehension may vary,
though the work apprehended be the same.   Thus,
one Christian, with little knowledge of his place in
Jesus, sees himself as still in the house of bondage;
but there, hiding within the blood-sprinkled door-posts,
he waits with girded loins to depart from Egypt.*
Another by faith sees further, even to the experience
of the wilderness, knowing that Pharaoh is judged,†
and the Red Sea behind him.   A third sees further
still, even into the land, and knows himself even now
over Jordan.‡   In a word, one sees Exodus, another
Numbers, another Joshua.   Yet the reality, though
differently apprehended, is the same,—salvation through
the blood of Jesus.   The difference is in our apprehension of it, and it is this difference that these books,
if regarded typically, are so full of.   It is, I believe,
precisely similar in these types of Christ in His work
as offering.   The different offerings give us the different aspects of His offering; the different grades
in the same offering, the different apprehensions of the
same aspect.

The truth is, that Christ's work is so manifold, and
has so many different aspects, and each aspect may be
so differently apprehended, according to the different

* Cf. 1 Peter i. 13, and Exod. xii. 11.
† John xii. 31.   ‡ Ephesians ii. 6.

measure of light in the believer, that one type or one history, however full, can never fully describe or represent Him. We see this unquestionably in the Gospels, in reference to the person of the Lord. One Gospel does not shew out all the glories of His person : the subject requires four distinct presentations. The Gospels are not mere supplementary narratives of Christ in one relation. Each gives a separate view of Him. Not of His work in saving,—this we get in the Epistles, —but of Himself, His perfect character, His blessed person.

I do not here enter into the distinctions of the Gospels, though few subjects of inquiry are more blessed, further than to refer to them in illustration of our subject, as shewing the way in which the Word is written. Take but Luke and John. In their narratives, as in the offerings, in each, as others have observed, we have a distinct aspect of Jesus. Luke gives Him as Son of Adam : John as Son of God. In the former of these, therefore, I read His "genealogy," His "conception" of Mary, His "birth" at Bethlehem ; His "increase in wisdom and stature," and His "subjection" to His earthly parents ; His "baptism," His "temptation" in the wilderness, and His "anointing with the Holy Ghost." In John not a word about matters of this sort, but "the Word which was with God, and was God." Take any event narrated by the two Evangelists, not to say the general tone and tenor of their writings, and see how perfectly each narrative will be in keeping with the distinct character of each particular Gospel.

Take, for instance, a scene familiar to most of us, the agony in the garden of Gethsemane. In Luke* we see Jesus, the suffering "Son of Adam," in all points, sin excepted, tempted as we are; saying, "Father, if Thou be willing, remove this cup from me." An angel appears strengthening Him. In an agony He prays more fervently. He seems to seek sympathy from His disciples: great drops of blood fall to the ground. Now turn to the same scene in John,† and mark the striking contrast. Not a word about His prayer or agony; not a word about strength ministered to Him by an angel; not a word of His drops of blood, or of His apparent longing for sympathy in His trial. Throughout He is "the Word" incarnate. "Jesus knowing all things that should come upon Him, went forth and said, Whom seek ye?" "As soon as He had said unto them, I am He, they went backward, and fell to the ground." Here, instead of weakness and agony, is power appalling His adversaries. Then again, instead of seeking sympathy from His disciples, He is seen rather as possessing the power to protect them. "If therefore ye seek me, let these go their way; that the saying might be fulfilled which He spake, Of those whom thou hast given me I have lost none."

Some saints see nothing of this. Like Israel in Egypt, the only truth for them is redemption. Little distinction can they see either in the work or offices of Jesus. Still less do they see of His character or person. But among those who do see these things, how vast

* Chapter xxii. 42. † Chapter xviii.

may be the difference of spiritual intelligence. It is this distinction, I cannot doubt, which is brought out, as the subject demands, in the varieties of the Offerings.

But it is time that we turn to THE BURNT-OFFERING. Let us examine it, first, *in its contrast to the other offerings;* and then, secondly, *in its varieties.*

I. IN ITS CONTRAST TO THE OTHER OFFERINGS, at least four points may be enumerated. It was, (1.) *A sweet savour offering,* and, (2.) *Offered for acceptance;* in these two particulars it differed from the Sin-offerings. (3.) Thirdly, it was *the offering of a life:* in this it differed from the Meat-offering. (4.) Fourthly, *it was wholly burnt;* here it differed from all, and particularly from the Peace-offering.

(1.) First, it was *a sweet savour* offering: "a sweet savour unto Jehovah."* I have already adverted to the difference between the offerings, and that they were divided into two great and distinctive classes,—first, the sweet savour offerings, which were all, as we shall find, oblations for acceptance; and secondly, those offerings which were not of a sweet savour, and which were required as an expiation for sin. The first class, the sweet savour offerings,—comprising the Burnt-offering, the Meat-offering, and the Peace-offering,†—were offered on the brazen altar which stood in the Court of the Tabernacle. The second class,—the Sin and Trespass-offerings,‡—were not consumed on the altar: some of them were burnt on the earth without the camp; others the

* Verses 9, 13, 17. † Chapters i. ii. iii.
‡ Chapters iv. v. vi.

priest ate, having first sprinkled the blood for atonement. In the first class, sin is not seen or thought of :
it is the faithful Israelite giving a sweet offering to
Jehovah. In the Sin-offerings it is just the reverse : it
is an offering charged with the sin of the offerer. Thus,
in the first class,—that is, the Burnt-offering, the Meat-
offering, and the Peace-offering,—the offerer came for
acceptance as a worshipper. In the second class, in the
Sin and Trespass-offerings, he came as a sinner to pay
the penalty of sin and trespass. In either case the
offering was without blemish; for the Sin-offerings
required perfectness in the victim as much as the Burnt-
offering. But in the one the offerer appears as man in
perfectness, and in his offering stands the trial of fire,—
that is, God's searching holiness; and accepted as a
fragrant savour, all ascends a sweet offering to Jehovah.
In the other, the offerer appears as a sinner, and in his
offering bears the penalty due to his offences.

Now the Burnt-offering was of the first class, a
sweet-smelling savour ; as such in perfect contrast with
the Sin-offerings. We are not here, therefore, to consider Christ as the Sin-bearer, but as man in perfectness meeting God in holiness. The thought here is
not, " God hath made Him to be sin for us," * but
rather, " He loved us, and gave Himself for us an
offering and a sacrifice to God of a sweet-smelling
savour." † Jesus, blessed be His name, both in the
Burnt-offering and Sin-offering, stood as our representative. When He obeyed, He obeyed "for us:" when

* 2 Cor. v. 21.   † Eph. v. 2.

He suffered, He suffered "for us." But in the Burnt-offering He appears *for us*, not as our sin-bearer, but as man offering to God something which is most precious to Him. We have here what we may in vain search for elsewhere;—man giving to God what truly satisfies Him. The thought here is not that sin has been judged, and that man in Christ has borne the judgment :—this would be the Sin-offering. The Burnt-offering shews us man going even further, and giving to God an offering so pleasing to Him that the sweet savour of it satisfies Him, and will satisfy Him for ever. With our experience of what man is, it seems wondrous that he should ever perfectly perform his part to God-ward. But in Christ man has so performed it : His offering was "a sweet savour unto the Lord."

Here, then, is the first thought presented to us in the Burnt-offering : God finds food, that is, satisfaction, in the offering. In other oblations we have Christ as the faithful Israelite, by His offering feeding and satisfying the priests. Here He is seen satisfying Jehovah. The altar is "the table of the Lord :"* whatever was put upon it was "the food of God."† The fire from heaven, emblem of God's holiness, consumes the offering ; and it all ascends as sweet incense before Him.‡ And just as in the Burnt-offering the

* Mal. i. 12.   † Lev. xxi. 6, 8, 17, 21, 22, margin.

‡ The word used for the Burnt-offering, עֹלָה, literally "*ascending*," is the same as that used for burning incense. The burning of the Sin-offering is expressed by an entirely different word.

D

fire from heaven fell and consumed the sacrifice of the altar,—a pledge to him who offered it that there was something in the offering which God found pleasure in, —so, typically speaking, did God find food in the unblemished sacrifice of Jesus. His perfect spotlessness and devotedness was a sweet feast to the God of heaven. Here was something according to His taste. Here, at least, He found satisfaction.

We too often omit this thought when thinking of the offering of Jesus. We think of His death; but little of His life. We look but little into His ways. Yet it is His ways throughout His pilgrimage, even to the way He laid down His life, which God so delights in. Our views are so selfish and meagre. If we are saved, we seek no further. Most saints, therefore, have very little thought of Christ's offering, except as offered for sin, "delivered for our offences." God, however, puts the Burnt-offering first: for this was peculiarly His portion in Jesus. And just in proportion as a believer grows in grace, we shall find him turning intelligently to the Gospels; from them adding to the knowledge he has of the work of Jesus greater knowledge of His ways and person; with earnest desire to know more of the Lord Himself, and how in all things He was "a sweet savour to Jehovah."

(2.) But the Burnt-offering was not only "a sweet savour;" it was also an offering *"for acceptance,"*— that is, it was offered to God to secure the acceptance of the offerer. So we read,—I give the more correct

translation,—"he shall offer it *for his acceptance.*"*
To understand this, we must recur for a moment to
the position Christ occupied as offerer. He stood for
man as man under the law, and, as under law, His
acceptance depended on His perfectness. God had
made man upright; but he had sought out many
inventions. One dispensation after another had tried
whether, under any circumstances, man could render
himself acceptable to God. But age after age passed
away: no son of Adam was found who could meet
God's standard. The law was man's last trial, whether,
with a revelation of God's mind, he could or would
obey it. But this trial, like the others, ended in
failure: "there was none righteous, no, not one."
How, then, was man to be reconciled to God? How
could he be brought to meet God's requirements?
One way yet remained, and the Son of God accepted
it. "He took not on Him the nature of angels; but He
took the seed of Abraham;" and in His person, once
and for ever, man was reconciled to God. In effecting
this, Jesus, as man's representative, took man's place,
where He found man, under law; and there, in obedience to the law, He offered, *"for His acceptance."*

* In the common version these words are translated, "He shall
offer it *of his own voluntary will.*" (Ver. 3.) The Septuagint, the
Chaldee version, the Vulgate, and the Targum Hierosolymitanum,
all render this, "*to be accepted;*" which is confirmed by ver. 4:—
"*it shall be accepted for him.*" The words are לִרְצֹנוֹ and וְנִרְצָה.
I may add, that the same expression, where it occurs in Lev. xxxiii.
11, is in our version also, as well as in those referred to, translated
"*to be accepted.*"

The question was, could man bring an offering **so** acceptable as to satisfy God? Jesus as man did bring such an offering. He offered Himself, and His offering was accepted. Even with our poor thoughts of what Jesus was to the Father, it seems wondrous that He, the Blessed One, should ever have thus offered "*for His acceptance.*" But this was only one of the many steps of humiliation which He took, as our representative, "for us."

And this explains the word "atonement" in the fourth verse :—"It shall be accepted for him *to make atonement.*" These words might suggest to some the thought of *sin* in connexion with the Burnt-offering. Such a view of the case would be erroneous. The word "*atonement*" here, as elsewhere, in itself means simply *making satisfaction :* and satisfaction may be of two sorts, depending on that which we have to satisfy. We may satisfy a loving and holy requirement, or satisfy offended justice. Either would be *satisfaction :* the Burnt-offering is the former ; the Sin-offering the latter.

And that the atonement of the Sin-offering is of **a** very different nature from the atonement here spoken of in the Burnt-offering, will at once be seen by any who will compare what is said of the atonement of the Burnt-offering and of the Sin-offerings : for in the Sin-offering we find it expressly added that the atonement is an "*atonement for the offerer's sin.*"* This

* See chap. iv. 20, 26, 31; chap. v. 6, 10, 13, 16, 18; chap. vi. **7;** where in every case the atonement of the Sin-offerings is expressly

is never said in the Burnt-offering : on the contrary, it is said to be " offered *for acceptance.*" The atonement of the Burnt-offering is the satisfaction which God receives from the perfectness which the offerer presents to Him. The atonement of the Sin-offering is expiatory : the offerer by his offering satisfies offended justice. In the Sin-offering the atonement is *for sin;* the offering, therefore, is not presented for acceptance ; but as seen charged with the sin of the offerer, is cast out, the victim of a broken law: thenceforth, as under the imputation of sin, and regarded as unfit for a place among God's people, it is cast out from the midst of Israel, and burnt without the camp. In the Burnt-offering the atonement is made by one who comes as a worshipper *without sin,* and in his sinless offering offers for acceptance that which is received as a sweet savour by the Lord. Man is under trial, indeed, and offering for acceptance: but he is seen accepted, as having satisfied God. I need not say that but One ever did this perfectly, and He gave Himself, and was accepted for us.*

(3.) The third point peculiar to the Burnt-offering was, that *a life was offered on the altar :*—" He shall kill the bullock before the Lord, and sprinkle the blood upon the altar." † In this particular the Burnt-offering stands distinguished from the Meat-offering, which in other respects it closely resembles. In the Meat-

connected with *sin.* There is nothing like this in the atonement of the Burnt-offering, chap. i. 4.

    * Eph. v. 2; Tit. ii. 14.   † Verse 5.

offering, however, the offering was "corn, oil, and frank-incense;" here the offering is *a life*. The right under-standing of the precise import of this particular will help us to the distinct character of the Burnt-offering. Life was that part in creation which from the begin-ning God claimed as His. As such,—as being His claim on His creatures,—it stands as an emblem for what we owe Him. What we owe to God is our duty to Him. And this, I doubt not, is the thought here intended. Of course, the offering here, as elsewhere, is the body of Jesus, that body which He took, and then gave for us: but in giving God *a life*, in contradistinction to offering Him corn or frankincense, the peculiar thought is the fulfilment of the first table of the Decalogue. Thus the life yielded is man's *duty to God*, and man here is seen perfectly giving it. Am I asked what man ever thus offered? I answer, none but One, "the man Christ Jesus." * He alone of all the sons of Adam in perfectness accomplished all man's duty to God-ward; He in His own blessed and perfect righteous-ness met every claim God could make upon Him. Again, I say, He did it "for us," and we are "accepted in Him."

(4.) The fourth and last feature peculiar to the Burnt-offering is, that *it was wholly burnt on the altar*. "The priest shall burn all upon the altar, to be a burnt sacrifice unto the Lord."† In this particular the Burnt-offering differed from the Meat and Peace-offerings, in which a part only was burnt with fire; nor did it differ

* 1 Tim. ii. 5.　　　　　† Verse 9.

less from those offerings for Sin, which, though wholly burnt, were not burnt upon the altar.

The import of this distinction is manifest, and in exact keeping with the character of the offering. Man's duty to God is not the giving up of one faculty, but the entire surrender of all. So Christ sums up the First Commandment,—all the mind, all the soul, all the affections. "Thou shalt love the Lord thy God with *all thy heart*, and with *all thy soul*, and with *all thy mind*."* I cannot doubt that the type refers to this in speaking so particularly of the parts of the Burnt-offering; for "the head," "the fat," "the legs," "the inwards," are all distinctly enumerated.† "The head" is the well-known emblem of *the thoughts;* "the legs" the emblem of *the walk;* and "the inwards" the constant and familiar symbol of *the feelings and affections of the heart.* The meaning of "the fat" may not be quite so obvious, though here also Scripture helps us to the solution.‡ It represents the energy not of one limb or faculty, but *the general health and vigour of the whole.* In Jesus these were all surrendered, and all without spot or blemish. Had there been but one thought in the mind of Jesus which was not perfectly given to God;—had there been but one affection in the heart of Jesus which was not yielded to His Father's will;—had there been one step in the walk of Jesus which was taken not for God, but for His own pleasure;—then He could not have offered Himself **or**

* Matt. xxii. 37.   † Verses 8, 9.
‡ Ps. xvii. 10, xcii. 14, cxix. 70; Deut. xxxii. 15.

been accepted as "a whole burnt-offering to Jehovah."
But Jesus gave up all : He reserved nothing. All was
burnt, all consumed upon the altar.

I do not know that there is anything more remarkable than this in the perfect offering of our blessed
Master. Everything He did or said was for God. From
first to last self had no place : His Father's work, His
Father's will, were everything. The first words recorded
of Him as a child are, "I must be about my Father's
business." His last words on the cross, "It is finished,"
proclaim how that business and that labour were
fulfilled and cared for. So entirely was His whole life
devoted to spend and be spent for His Father, that in
reading the Gospels the thought scarce occurs to us
that He could have had a will of His own. Yet Jesus
was perfect man, and as such had a human will as we
have. In one point only did it differ from ours : His
will was always subject to His Father. As a man, His
thoughts were human thoughts; His affections human
affections. But how much of these did He reserve for
self, for His own ease, or credit, or pleasure ? What
one act recorded of Him was for His own advancement ?
What one word which was not in entire devotedness to
His Father ?

But it is vain to endeavour to describe His perfectness ; words cannot express it : God only knows it.
Of this, however, I am fully assured,—the more we are
in communion with God, the more we shall estimate it.
Out of God's presence we see no beauty in Jesus : His
very perfectness is so strange to our natural judgments.

Had He been less devoted, we should have better understood Him. Nay, had His self-surrender been less complete, we should have valued it higher. Had He, instead of always refusing to be anything here, taken the glory of the world for a season, and then resigned it, we should probably have thought more of His humiliation in becoming the friend and companion of the poor. But so it was, and so it is still; the more humble, the more despised in man's eyes; the more faithful, the less accepted. But the Burnt-offering was for God's acceptance, not for man's. He at least could estimate the full value of the offering.

Such was *"the whole burnt-*offering:"* the entire surrender of self to God in everything. How utterly in contrast to what the world thinks wisdom; "for men will praise thee when thou doest well to thyself."* Nay, how utterly unlike anything which can be found even in believers. With us how many thoughts are there for self; for *our* ease, *our* pleasure, *our* interest. How much of our walk, how much of our affections, is consumed on anything rather than the altar! It was not so with the blessed Jesus. "With all His heart" He lived for God, for "the inwards" were all consumed: "with all His soul and with all His strength," for "the fat and head" were offered. His offering was not the surrender of one part, while He kept what He most valued for Himself. It was not the surrender of what cost nothing, or what cost but little, or what was com-

* Psalm xlix. 18.

paratively worthless. "He gave Himself," * in all His perfectness, and satisfied the heart of God.

Such is the general aspect of the Burnt-offering, as distinguished from the other offerings. It was *a sweet savour, an offering for acceptance, the offering of a life,* and *wholly burnt upon the altar.* Let us now proceed to examine,

II. ITS VARIETIES, that is, the different measures of apprehension with which it may be seen.

There were, then, three grades in the Burnt-offering. It might be "*of the herd,*"† or "*of the flock,*"‡ or "*of fowls.*"§ These different grades gave rise to several varieties in the offering, the import of which we shall now consider.

(1.) The first difference is in *the animal offered.* We have in the first grade, "*a bullock ;*" in the second, "*a lamb;*" in the third, "*a turtle-dove.*" Each of these animals, from their well-known character, presents us with a different thought respecting the offering. *The bullock,* "strong to labour," ‖—for "great increase is by the strength of the ox," ¶—suggests at once the thought of service, of patient, untiring labour. In *the lamb* we have another picture presented to us; here the thought is passive submission without a murmur: for the lamb is the figure constantly chosen to represent the submissive, uncomplaining character of Christ's sufferings. "He was led as a lamb to the slaughter, and as a sheep before her shearer is dumb, so He open-

* Eph. v. 2.   † Verse 3.   ‡ Verse 10.   § Verse 14.
‖ Ps. cxliv. 4.   ¶ Prov. xiv. 4.

eth not his mouth." * The *turtle-dove* is different from
either of these, and gives again another view of the
offering of Jesus.   In this class the thought of labour
is lost sight of: the unmurmuring submission, too, of
the lamb is wanting: the thought is rather simply one
of mourning innocence; as it is written, "We mourn
like doves;" † and again, "Be harmless as doves." ‡

Here, then, are some of the measures of apprehension with which the sacrifice of Jesus as Burnt-offering
may be regarded; for a saint may see either His devoted labour, His uncomplaining submission, or His
mourning innocence.   All these are equally true, all
equally precious, all equally acceptable : yet all do not
equally bring out the distinct character of this perfect
offering.   The thought of the Burnt-offering, as we
have already seen, is man fulfilling his duty towards
God.   But man's duty to God is not merely a life of
innocence, or a life of submission; it is also a life of
labour.   "The bullock" brings out this thought distinctly: the other classes, "the lamb" and "turtle-dove,"
omit it.

It may be asked, what do we learn by "*the goat*," §
which was sometimes offered in one of the lower grades
of the Burnt-offering?   If I mistake not, this emblem
suggests a thought of the Sin-offering, reminding us of
Christ's offering as scape-goat.   This view of the case
may seem to be open to an objection; and I may be
asked how the thought of sin can be connected with

* Isa. liii. 7.   † Isa. lix. 11, xxxviii. 14.
‡ Matt. x. 16.   § Verse 10.

the Burnt-offering? I answer, these different grades in the offerings are but different *measures of apprehension;* and there may be apprehension enough to see Christ bringing His offering, without clearly distinguishing the different aspects of that offering. Accordingly, we find that in the lower grades of all the offerings, the distinctive character of the particular offering is constantly lost sight of, while a thought or view of some other offering is partially substituted in its place.*
This is what we might naturally have expected as the result of a smaller measure of apprehension. It is what we find universally the case in those whose views of Christ are limited. So in the type; where the measure of apprehension is small, there is a confusion between two different aspects of Christ's offering. The building, to recur to a former illustration, is viewed from so great a distance, that more than one side of it is seen, though neither of the sides is seen very distinctly. Thus with many the thought of Jesus as Burnt-offering is scarce distinguished from the thought of the Sin-offering. These different relations of His work are unseen, or at least they are very much confused together.

Such are some of the varieties of the Burnt-offering, corresponding to the different apprehensions which be-

---

* This is seen especially in the last grade of the Meat-offering, and in the last two grades of the Sin-offering. The last class of the Meat-offering gives us a thought of "first-fruits;" (chap. ii. 14.) The last grade but one of the Sin-offering is seen as "a sweet savour" Burnt-offering; (chap. iv. 31;) while the last grade of all is represented as almost a Meat-offering; (chap. v. 11, 12.)

lievers have of Jesus: for His offering may be seen as the bullock, the lamb, the goat, or the turtle-dove. Comparatively few, I believe, see Jesus as presented in the first class,—the patient, unwearied labourer for others. The lamb, the goat, the turtle-dove, are all more familiar symbols. The fact is, we need to be ourselves in service, and to know practically something of its toil and trial, before we can at all rightly estimate the aspect of Christ's offering which is presented in the emblem of the bullock. The Gospels, however, are full of this view of the Burnt-offering: in fact, one whole Gospel is specially devoted to it. In Mark, Jesus is not brought before us as in the other Gospels, either as Son of Abraham, Son of Adam, or Son of God; He stands rather,—as another has observed,—the patient, untiring labourer for others. In Mark, turn where we will, we see Jesus always " the girded servant;" always at the disposal of others, to spend and be spent at their bidding. Thus when, after days of ceaseless labour, He retires alone for prayer or rest with His disciples, no sooner do the multitude disturb Him than He at once goes with them, or rises to minister to their need.* So entirely does He give Himself to His work, that " He had no leisure so much as to eat;"† but He had meat to eat which the world saw not: "His meat was to do His Father's will."‡ And oh, what touches of grace are there in all His service! He not only cures the blind, but " He takes

* Mark i. 35–38, vi. 30–45; &c. &c.
† Mark iii. 20, vi. 31.   ‡ John iv. 31–34.

him by the hand." *   He not only raises the dead:
His mission in that house ends not till, with careful
foresight, "He commands them to give her meat." †
Blessed Lord, shew us more of Thy footsteps, that,
while we rejoice in Thy work, we may learn to follow
Thee.

(2.) A second distinction between the different grades
of the Burnt-offering is, that while *in the first grade
the parts are discriminated, in the last this peculiarity
is omitted:* the bird was killed, *but not divided.*   In
the case of the bullock and the lamb, it is noticed that
the offering is "cut into its pieces."   Here "the legs,
the head, the fat, the inwards," are all distinctly
noticed and enumerated.‡   In the last case, that of
the turtle-dove, it is otherwise: "he shall not divide it
asunder." §   "The legs, the head, the inwards," as we
have already seen, represent the walk, the thoughts,
the feelings of Jesus.   In the first grade these are all
apprehended: they are all lost sight of in the last.
These grades represent, as I have said, measures of
apprehension.   Where the measure of spiritual apprehension is large, a saint will see the offering dissected:
his eyes will be turning constantly to see the walk, the
mind, the affections of Jesus.   He will now observe,
what once he regarded not, how Jesus walked, how He
thought, what were His feelings.   On the other hand,
where Jesus is but little apprehended, all the details of
His walk and feelings will be unseen.   Christ's charac-

* Mark viii. 23.   † Mark v. 43.
‡ Verses 6, 8, 9.   § Verse 17.

ter will not be dissected, nor the different parts of His work appear.

It is further noticed in the type, that, in the first class of the Burnt-offering, " *the inwards and legs were washed in water.*"* Nothing like this is seen in the last grade: there even the parts are not discriminated. What are we to learn by this distinction? " *The legs*" and " *the inwards*" are the walk and affections. " *The water* " represents the Spirit acting through the Word; as it is written, " Christ loved the church, and gave Himself for it; that He might sanctify and cleanse it *by the washing of water by the Word;* " † and again,—" Sanctify them through Thy truth; *Thy word is truth.*" ‡ Christ, though without spot or blemish, yet as a man in His feelings and walk submitted to God's Word and Spirit. As a man He was Himself sanctified by them; for as He said, " By the word of Thy lips I have kept me."§ The law said, " Man shall not live by bread alone, but by every word of God ;" ‖ and Jesus, as man, fully did so: every step, every feeling, obeyed. But all this is lost sight of in the turtle-dove. The discrimination of the parts, and the washing of water, are both unnoticed.

(3.) A third distinction between the different grades of the Burnt-offering is, that while *in the first grade the offerer is seen to lay his hand on the offering,*¶ *in the other grades this act is not observed.* I have

---

* Verse 9.   † Eph. v. 26, τῷ λουτρῷ τοῦ ὕδατος, ἐν ῥήματι.
‡ John xvii. 17.   § Psalm xvii. 4.
‖ Deut. viii. 3 ; Luke iv. 4.   ¶ Verse 4.

already adverted to the import of this action as repre-
senting the identity of the offering and offerer. In the
first grade of the Burnt-offering this identity is seen:
it is wholly lost sight of in the other grades. Not a
few see Christ as offering for us, without fully realising
that His offering was *Himself*. They see that He gave
up this thing or that; that He gave much for us, and
that what He gave was most precious. But they do
not really see that "*He gave Himself*," that His own
blessed person was what He offered. This is clearly
seen in the first grade of the Burnt-offering. It is lost
sight of, or unobserved, in the other grades.

(4.) A fourth distinction, closely allied with the one
just considered, is, that *in the first class the offerer is
seen to kill the victim,—in the last the priest kills it.**
In fact, in the last class, the priest does nearly everything, the offerer is scarcely seen at all; whereas in
the first class it is just the reverse, there are many
particulars noted of the offerer. The import of this
is at once obvious, when we see the distinction between
the priest and offerer. The *offerer,* as I have already
observed, sets Christ before us *in His person.* The
priest represents Him *in His official character,* as the
appointed Mediator between God and man. Where
the identity between the offerer and offering is apprehended, the offerer is seen to kill the offering; that is,
Christ is seen in His person, of His own will laying
down His life; as it is written,—" No man taketh
it from me, but I lay it down of myself." † On the

---

* Compare verses 5 and 15.   † John x. 18.

contrary, where the identity of the offering and offerer is unseen or disregarded, the priest is seen to kill the victim, that is, Christ's death is seen as the work of the Mediator; and is connected with *His official character* as Priest, rather than with *His person* as the willing Offerer. So with believers, where there is only a limited measure of apprehension, little is known of Christ save *His office* as Mediator: He Himself, *His blessed person*, is overlooked or but little seen.

Such are the chief varieties of the Burnt-offering: how full are they of instruction to the believer: how clearly do they mark the different apprehensions among saints respecting the work and person of our Lord. Some, however,—I speak of believers,—are content to know nothing of this; and they would rather not be told their ignorance. They can see but one truth,—the Paschal lamb,—and anything further they neither care nor wish for. Such, whether they are aware of it or not, shew too plainly that they know little either of the wilderness or of the tabernacle, that hitherto their home has been Egypt, and that as yet they are little better than bondsmen there. But after through grace we are out of Egypt, and have received a knowledge of the varied offerings; after we know and are assured of our deliverance, and have spiritual apprehension enough to see the different aspects of Christ's offering; how much remains to be learnt of Jesus in any or every aspect of His work. There are babes as well as strong men in the wilderness, and the babes can know but little till they are grown. Yea, there are men of

Israel, full-grown men, in the wilderness, who through unfaithfulness are almost strangers to the offering. With all such the measure of apprehension will be limited, and consequently their joy and strength but small. Lord, awaken Thy saints to know their calling, by knowing more and more of Jesus; that instead of boasting themselves as children of Abraham, while they are bondsmen in Babylon or Egypt, they may seek as sons of Abraham to walk as he did, as strangers and pilgrims with Thee!

Here I conclude my remarks on the Burnt-offering. In it we have seen Jesus as *our representative.* His offering was offered "for us;" therefore "as He is, so are we in this world;"* the measure of His acceptance is the measure of our acceptance,—"we are made accepted in the Beloved."† But in the Burnt-offering Jesus stands also as *our example,* "leaving us an example that we should follow His steps;"‡ the measure therefore of His devotedness should be the measure of ours,—"we should walk even as He walked." §

May the Lord grant to His Church more fully to know and apprehend her calling, her union with Jesus dead and risen, and her hope when He appears; that so while she rejoices in her inheritance, and that Jesus represents her above, she may daily be found nearer to His cross, and more and more represent Him here. Amen.

* 1 John iv. 17.   † Eph. i. 6.
‡ 1 Peter ii. 21.   § 1 John ii. 6.

THE MEAT-OFFERING.

LEVITICUS II.

WE now come to THE MEAT-OFFERING, which gives us
another aspect of the perfect offering of Jesus. We
may consider it, first, *in its contrasts to the other
offerings;* that is, as giving us one definite and particular aspect of His offering: and then, secondly, *in
its several varieties;* that is, as bringing out the
different apprehensions of this one aspect.

I. And first, IN ITS CONTRAST TO THE OTHER OFFER-
INGS. Five points here at once present themselves,
which bring out what is distinctive in this offering
The apprehension of these will enable us to see *the
particular relation* which Jesus filled for man as
Meat-offering.

(1.) The first point is that the Meat-offering was *a
sweet savour.** In this particular it stands in contrast
to the Sin-offering, but in exact accordance with the
Burnt-offering. For this latter reason I need not
dwell upon the purport of it, as I have already sufficiently considered it in the Burnt-offering. Suffice it

* Chapter ii. 2, 9.

to say, that the thought of sin never comes into any of the sweet savour offerings : they represent man in perfect obedience yielding to God an offering which He accepts as pleasing to Him. The Sin-offerings, on the contrary, are not a sweet savour : they represent man as a sinner receiving the penalty due to his offences. But I have already sufficiently pointed out this distinction. I do not therefore here further dwell upon it.

(2.) The second point in which the Meat-offering differed from the others, is seen in *the materials* of which it was composed. These were "*flour, oil, and frankincense :*"* there is no giving up of *life* here. It is in this particular, especially, that the Meat-offering differs from the Burnt-offering. The question is, does the Scripture supply us with a key by which to discover what is intended by this distinction ? That it does so, not on this point alone, but on every other, I do not entertain a doubt. The Scripture is a key to itself. Besides, we have the Holy Ghost to open it to us : and especially is this His office where Jesus is the subject of our inquiries. God is His own interpreter. We fail in understanding the Scripture because we so little use Him. This I feel assured is the reason we are so often in ignorance. It is not that the truth sought for is not in the Word, but that through lack of communion with Him who gave that Word, we have not enough of His mind to apprehend His meaning, even where He has fully expressed it.

* Verse 1.

But to return. I said that the great distinction between the Burnt-offering and the Meat-offering was, that *life* was offered in the one case, *fruits* in the other. The key to this I believe may be found in more than one place in Scripture. Thus in the first chapter of Genesis we read of God thus allotting to man that part of creation which He intended to satisfy him:—"Behold, I have given you *every herb* bearing seed, which is upon the face of all the earth, and *every tree* in which is the fruit of a tree yielding seed ; *to you it shall be for meat.*" * Thus *the fruit* of the herb and of the tree was man's allotted portion. But *life* was reserved as God's portion, and wholly belonged to Him. It was only after the flood, (and this too I believe is typical,) that man was permitted to eat the flesh of animals. Yet even then the *life* was God's part: as it is written, "The life, which is the blood, ye shall not eat." †

The import of this difference between the Burnt and Meat-offerings may now be surely and easily gathered. Life is that which from the beginning God claimed as His part in creation : as an emblem, therefore, it represents what the creature owes to God. Corn, the fruit of the earth, on the other hand, is man's part in creation ; as such, it stands the emblem of man's claim, or of what we owe to man. What we owe to God or to man is respectively our duty to either. Thus in the Burnt-offering the surrender of life to God represents the fulfilment of man's duty to God ; man yielding to

* Genesis i. 29.   † Genesis ix. 4.

God His portion to satisfy all His claim. In the Meat-offering the gift of corn and oil represents the fulfilment of man's duty to his neighbour : man in his offering surrendering himself to God, but doing so that he may give to man his portion. Thus the Burnt-offering is the perfect fulfilment of the laws of the first table ; the Meat-offering the perfect fulfilment of the second. Of course, in both cases the offering is but one,—that offering is "the body" of Jesus ; but that body is seen offered in different aspects : here in the Meat-offering as fulfilling man's duty to man. The one case is man satisfying God, giving Him His portion, and receiving testimony that it is acceptable. The other is man satisfying his neighbour, giving man his portion as an offering to the Lord.

And how exactly do the emblems here chosen represent the perfect fulness of this blessed offering. God's claim met perfectly in the Burnt-offering : man's claim as perfectly satisfied here. Had the Burnt-offering alone been offered, man would have lacked his portion and been unsatisfied : and again, had the Meat-offering been offered to the exclusion of the Burnt-offering, God would have been unsatisfied ; it would have been imperfect. But it could not be so ; therefore after the law came in, the Meat-offering was regarded as an adjunct of the Burnt-offering. Thus the book of Numbers always speaks of the Meat-offering as in use and practice connected with the Burnt-offering. Having first regulated the amount of flour for the Meat-offering, which was to accompany the different classes of the

Burnt-offering,* the law proceeds to speak of "the Burnt-offering and *its* Meat-offering," "the Burnt-offering and the Meat-offering *thereof*." † So again in Ezra the offerings for the altar are summed up as "bullocks, rams, lambs, with *their* Meat-offerings." ‡

The Meat-offering was in fact Cain's offering, but offered by one who had first offered as Abel did. Cain's offering was "the fruit of the ground," offered to God without bloodshedding. How could this, the mere acknowledgment of man's claim, satisfy Him who had His own claim also on His creatures? And this was Cain's error. Here was a fallen man, through the fall an exile from Eden, despising the sprinkled blood, that is, the acknowledgment of God's claim upon him; and presuming to approach and satisfy God with the fruit of the earth, that is, man's claim. Yet how many, even now, are thinking to render Cain's offering, deceiving themselves with the idea that of itself it will be accepted. Had any man's service to his fellow-creatures been such as to justify him before God, that one would have been our blessed Lord; yet even He came not without a Burnt-offering. Christ's perfect fulfilment of every duty to man was not enough without entire devotedness, even to death, to God-ward. Nor could all this perfectness avail for sinners, had not the Perfect One further been judged for sin.

The Meat-offering, then, to speak of it generally, is Christ presenting Himself to God as man's meat. Most

* Numb. xxviii. 12, 13.   † Numb. xxix., *passim.*
‡ Ezra vii. 17; see also Judges xiii. 19.

sweet it is, most precious to the soul of the believer who can thus see Jesus. We shall see this preciousness as we examine particularly the typical import of each of the materials of the Meat-offering.

[i.] The first is "*flour;*" and the type is significant, in exact accordance with the word, "Bread corn must be bruised."* Bread is the staff of life, and Christ our staff of life is here represented as the bruised One. The emblem, corn ground to powder, is one of the *deepest suffering.* It is not the blade springing up in beauty, green and flourishing with the rain of heaven, or ripening into full maturity under the influence of the summer sun. The thought is one of bruising and grinding; of pressing, wearing trial. Jesus was not only tried by "*fire;*" God's holiness was not the only thing that consumed Him. In meeting the wants of man, His blessed soul was grieved, and pressed and bruised continually. And the bruising here was from those to whom He was ministering, for whom He daily gave Himself. Who can read the Gospels without seeing this? Jesus lays Himself out for others; He spends Himself for others; but they cannot understand Him. His soul is grieved, His spirit bruised with the blindness and hardness of their hearts.

Oh, what a picture of devotedness does His lowly service present to us! Look at Him beginning His course, knowing each sorrow that was to befall Him; foreseeing the whole course of rejection, and the shameful end of His pilgrimage: rejected when He would

* Isaiah xxviii. 28.

minister blessing; misunderstood when He gave instruction; suffering not merely at the hands of enemies, but more acutely from those around Him;—to them alone He said, "How long shall I suffer you?"*— rejected, misunderstood, suffering, He goes forward without the slightest faltering; He never stops for a moment in His devoted service to all around Him. To the very end of His course, as at the beginning, He is the meat of all who need and will accept Him. We think when trouble or sorrow comes on us, that it is time to care for ourselves. Not so Jesus. We think there must be a limit to our self-sacrifice. Not so our blessed Lord. We think that our interests, our credit, or at least our life, must not be touched or endangered. We think when our kindness is rejected we need not repeat it; we think our times of rest and relaxation are our own. Oh, how unlike to us in all was our blessed, lowly Master! Oh, how far above us in all things! Nothing moved His steadfast heart, or turned Him from doing good. In vain was the stupidity of His disciples, the rage of His enemies, or the craft of Satan. Jesus never wavered nor hesitated; His course of self-surrender was complete.

But are we to suppose He did not feel all this? God only knows the measure of His sufferings, or how deeply He was bruised and broken. As a man He was "in all points tempted as we are, yet without sin;" this aggravated His sufferings. The Psalms here and there give us a glance of His sorrows, though no murmur ever

* Mark ix. 19.

escaped His lips. "Reproach," He says, "has broken my heart. They lay to my charge things I know not. It was not an enemy that did this, for then I could have borne it: neither was it he that hated me that did magnify himself against me, for then I would have hid myself from him; but it was thou, a man mine equal, my guide, and mine acquaintance. We took sweet counsel together, and walked to the house of God in company."* It may be, some of God's children cannot enter into this; they know not as yet the trials of service. Only let them follow Jesus in spending and being spent for others, and the emblem of this type, "bruised corn," will not be altogether strange to them. And, indeed, how much is there of Christ's suffering which we have no idea of until through grace we are in measure brought into His circumstances, and feel the bruising which our brethren, oft unconsciously, inflict on us, while we would minister to, and be spent for them.

I have just glanced at some of the bruisings of Christ's spirit, but as respects His body also how much was He bruised! What labours, what pains, what weaknesses did He suffer to feed others!† So much was He worn by labour, that He could not even bear His cross. Another was compelled to bear it for Him.‡ Doubtless this was not kindness but necessity. Jesus was already ground and broken. He was now ready to be put upon the altar.

* Psalm lxix. 20, xxxv. 11, lv. 12, 13.
† Ps. xxii. 15, cii. 4, 5.   ‡ Mark xv. 21.

And what a lesson is there here for the believer who wishes to give himself in service to his brethren! This scripture, as in fact all Scripture, testifies that service is self-surrender, self-sacrifice. Christ, to satisfy others, was broken: and bread corn must still be bruised: and the nearer our ministry approaches the measure of His ministry,—immeasurably far as we shall ever be behind Him,—the more shall we resemble Him, the bruised, the oppressed, the broken One.

But there is another thought brought out in this emblem. The Meat-offering was not only flour; it was to be "*fine* flour."* In fine flour there is *no unevenness*, fit emblem of what Jesus was. In Him there was no unevenness. Perhaps in no one respect does He stand out more in contrast to His best and most beloved servants. Jesus was always even, always the same, unchanged by circumstances. In Him one day's walk never contradicted another, one hour's service never clashed with another. In Him every grace was in its perfectness, none in excess, none out of place, none wanting. Firm, unmoved, elevated, He was yet the meek, the gentle, the humble One. In Him firmness never degenerated into obstinacy, or calmness into stoical indifference. His gentleness never became a weakness, or His elevation of soul forgetfulness of others. With us our very graces are uneven, and clash and jostle with each other. Our very attempts to live and die for Him who loved us only shew how unlike Him we are.

* Verse 1.

Take His most devoted followers, a Paul, a John, a Peter. In each of them there is unevenness, one grace preponderates; in Paul energy, in Peter zeal, in John affection. And even in their very graces we see their failings. Paul's energy leads him to Macedonia when a door is opened in Troas :* he repents of his letter to Corinth, and then again he does not repent.† Peter too, through zeal, once and again takes a place he has not grace to occupy : he steps out on the water and sinks ;‡ he follows Jesus but to deny Him.§ So, too, in the beloved disciple, his very affection to his Master does but bring out his unlikeness to Him : he would be the highest, next to His Lord, in the kingdom ; ‖ he would call down fire on all who dared to reject Him.¶

And to turn from apostles to ourselves, we need not, I think, be shewn our unevenness. One thing when alone before God, we are quite another thing before our brethren. In solitude striving and praying against the very folly we commit in public. In one circumstance backward, in another hasty ; in this place steadfast, in that wavering. Nor is it our sins alone which shew our unevenness : our very graces are uneven : and our possessing one more than another only shews our deficiency. Why is it that in Paul, John, and Peter, we mark one grace peculiarly, while such a thought never so much as occurs to us in considering our blessed Lord ? Is it that His servants surpassed Him

* 1 Cor. ii. 12, 13.
† 2 Cor. vii. 8.
‡ Matt. xiv. 28–31.
§ Matt. xxvi. 58, &c.
‖ Matt. xx. 20–24.
¶ Luke ix. 54.

in energy, or zeal, or tenderness? The reason is, Jesus
was perfect. In His devotedness there was no unevenness. No one grace to be singled out where everything
and all were perfect.

[ii.] The next material in the Meat-offering is *oil.*
"He shall pour oil upon it;"* this was a necessary
ingredient: without it the offering was incomplete.
The typical signification of this will be familiar to
many, for the New Testament is full of allusions to it.
Oil, in its nature nourishing and healing, is the constant emblem of the Spirit's actings. Jesus as the
obedient man was filled with the Holy Ghost, and His
oblation of Himself as Meat-offering was in the unction
and power of the Spirit. Luke, the Gospel of the Son
of Man, gives abundant information on this point.
Accordingly we read,—when His public ministry commenced, when, to speak typically, He began to bring
His Meat-offering,—"*the Holy Ghost* descended on Him
visibly,"† the oil was poured on the flour. Immediately
after,‡ we read again, "Jesus, *full of the Holy Ghost,*
returned from Jordan." Again, in the fourteenth verse,
"Jesus returned *in the power of the Spirit* into Galilee."
Then immediately,§ in the synagogue of Nazareth,
when the book of the prophet Esaias is delivered to
Him, He finds the place which describes His anointing
and its consequences: and whether He heals the sick,
teaches the poor, or feeds the hungry, it is all done in
the power of the anointing. "*The Spirit of the Lord*

* Verse 1.   † Luke iii. 22.
‡ Luke iv. 1.   § Verse 16.

is upon me, because the Lord hath anointed me to preach the gospel to the poor, and to heal the broken-hearted." "God anointed Jesus of Nazareth with *the Holy Ghost* and power; and He went about doing good;"* this is exactly the Meat-offering. And the Gospels from one end to the other in every page are full of it. To take one example from the chapter referred too : no sooner had our Lord commenced His ministry, than they rose up and thrust Him out of the city.† Go where He would, He was still the Meat-offering ; the bruised corn and the oil are always together.

What a contrast to us in all this is Jesus our blessed Master! In Him, viewed simply as a man, the bruised corn is fully anointed. For this reason, bruised as He may be, He never lacks power. How different with us! We are not bruised, we are not broken, but we are powerless : and what little is attempted or done for others is too often in the energy of our flesh rather than in the power of the Spirit. It is this which so ruins our efforts ; the power we use for God is our power, not the Spirit. If "we go about doing good," is it, I ask, in the power of the anointing from above, or in the power derived from some earthly advantage of circumstance, or station, or natural ability? Is it not thought right to seek these things to give power where we feel power is wanting? But this is not the strength Christ walked in : the Meat-offering was " *anointed with oil.*"

* Acts x. 38.   † Luke iv. 29.

The truth is, that the greatest zeal and knowledge are useless towards others without the Spirit. Look at Christ's last interview with His disciples!* We read, "He opened their understandings that they might understand the Scriptures:" He then shewed them "what was written in the law of Moses, and in the prophets, and in the psalms concerning Him." He tells them further, that of these very truths they are the constituted "witnesses." He then "lifts up His hands and blesses them." Are they then fitly equipped for the work appointed them? No:—He says, "Tarry till ye be endued with power." They have knowledge of Christ, they have His commission, they have His blessing; but they lack power, and the word is, "Tarry." They must wait for "power from on high," and that power is the Spirit. When shall we learn that we require not only truth but power: and that the only power which avails in ministry is the power of the Holy Ghost?

I have one other remark to make here. The "oil" is in the Meat-offering, not in the Burnt-offering. In the Burnt-offering we have the Spirit as "water:"† in the Meat-offering it is seen as "oil." It is in relation to man, in service to our neighbour, that the Spirit is specially needed in *grace* and *power*. There is the flesh in our brethren to try us, and the thousand difficulties of intercourse with evil. How is this to be met aright, save in the grace and unction of the Spirit? But could Jesus in His offering of Himself be so

---

* Luke xxiv. 44–49.   † Chapter i. 9, and see page 63.

dependent as to need this anointing?   Could He require
the Spirit of power for His walk and service to those
around Him?   Yes, He humbled Himself even to this,
to take, as a lowly dependent man, the grace which He
manifested to others.   Blessed Jesus!   May we learn
more and more to be dependent like Thee.

[iii.] The third ingredient of the Meat-offering is
frankincense :—" he shall put frankincense thereon ;"*
in connexion with which, and yet in contrast, it is
commanded,—"ye shall burn *no honey* unto the Lord."†
These emblems, like all the others, are at once simple
yet most significant.   Frankincense is the most precious
of perfumes, of enduring and delightful fragrance : fit
emblem of the sweetness and fragrance of the offering of our blessed Lord.   Honey, on the other hand,
though sweet, is corruptible ; soon fermented, and
easily turned sour.   In frankincense the full fragrance
is not brought out until the perfume is submitted to
the action of fire.   In honey it is just the reverse ; the
heat ferments and spoils it.

The bearing of this on the offering of Jesus is
too obvious to require comment.   The fire of God's
holiness tried Him, but all was precious fragrance.
The holiness of God only brought out graces which
would have escaped our notice had He never suffered.
Yea, much of the precious odour of His offering was
the very result of His fiery trial.   How different is it in
believers!   There is in many a sweetness of nature,—
very sweet for a while it may seem to our taste,—which

* Verse 1.   † Verse 11.

yet will not stand the test of fire: the first trial is enough to sour it. Who is there that has been cast into sifting circumstances, where God's holiness and our ease or interests have come into collision, without feeling how much there is in us which could not be a sweet savour on the altar? And have we never found, in setting even before saints some plain but neglected command of our Master, that much of the sweetness in them, which we have taken to be frankincense, has at once shewn itself to be fermenting honey. It was not so with the blessed Jesus:—" Anointed with the oil of gladness above His fellows, all His garments smell of myrrh, aloes, and cassia."* " Because of the savour of His good ointments, His name is like ointment poured forth."† Sweetness there is in abundance, but the sweetness of frankincense, not honey. Well might the bride exclaim, " My beloved is a bundle of myrrh; my beloved is to me as clusters of camphire."‡ And not *to* her alone: *for* her He has been a sweet savour unto Jehovah.

[iv.] The fourth and last ingredient of the Meat-offering is *salt*:—" Every oblation of the meat-offering shalt thou season with salt."§ And to bring out the typical import more clearly, another emblem by way of contrast is added:—" No meat-offering shall be made with *leaven*:"|| there must be salt; there must be no leaven.

The import of these emblems is obvious: the one

* Psalm xlv. 7, 8.
† Canticles i. 3.
‡ Canticles i. 13, 14.
§ Verse 13.
|| Verse 11.

F

positively, the other negatively, bringing but one and the same thought before us. "Salt," the well-known preservative against corruption, is the emblem of perpetuity and incorruptness; while "leaven," on the other hand, composed of sour and corrupting dough, is the as well-known emblem of corruption. Thus, when the Apostle would sum up in a word "the incorruptness, gravity, and sincerity," befitting a Christian, he says, "Let your speech be always with grace, seasoned with salt." [*] Thus again, when a covenant is described as perpetual, it is spoken of as "a covenant of salt." [†] The use of the word "leaven" is even more familiar. We read of "the leaven of the Pharisees," [‡] "the leaven of the Sadducees," [§] and "the leaven of Herod." [||] So, too, in the Epistles, we are enjoined to "purge out the old leaven." [¶] Here we have a key to these emblems. Jesus in His blessed offering brought that with it which not only secured its own incorruption, but which supplied a preservative against corruption to whatever He might come in contact with. It

---

[*] Col. iv. 6.　　　　　[†] Numb. xviii. 19; 2 Chron. xiii. 5.
[‡] Luke xii. 1.　　　§ Matt. xvi. 6.　　　|| Mark viii. 15.
[¶] 1 Cor. v. 7. The parable of the leaven, Matt. xiii. 33, may perhaps be quoted as giving to leaven another meaning. I am satisfied, however, that there, as in every other place, leaven is the emblem of evil and corruption. Of course, the great thought in the parable is the spread of nominal Christianity, while it is left for spiritual apprehension to discern whether what is actually spread is good or evil. But the Church is so blind to her own state, that she can neither see it as foretold in Scripture or existing in fact. As with the disciples at the sepulchre, a fact is before us which but few have eyes or heart to apprehend.

might not always be sweet to man's taste, but it was
the seasoning of the offering to the Lord.

How different is it with the most devoted Christians!
Leaven is mixed with their choicest offerings. But
our God has foreseen and provided for it. Thus at
the offering at Pentecost, and the oblation with the
Peace-offering, (appointed emblems of the Church's
offering,) leavened cakes were offered to the Lord, but
though accepted, they could not be burnt as a sweet
savour. These offerings I shall notice as I proceed; I
do not therefore here enter into them, further than to
observe, that no measure of oil, that is, the Spirit, could
counteract the effect of leaven. A cake might be
anointed again and again, but if there had been leaven
in its composition, it could not be put upon the altar.
What a lesson for those who are looking to the Spirit
in them rather than to Christ for them as the ground
of acceptance! The Spirit's operations in the greatest
power will never alter or destroy the old nature. As
soon may we expect the nettle to yield us olives as for
sinful flesh to be ought but sinful. Salt water cannot
be washed sweet: you may pour oil on it, but they will
not mingle; "that which is born of the flesh is flesh;
that which is born of the Spirit is spirit."* The flesh
is still in Paul, after he has been caught up to Paradise;
he therefore needs the thorn in it to humble him.†
The power of the flesh in us may be controlled, and its
active energy restrained or weakened, but the leaven is
still within us, only waiting its opportunity to rise.

* John iii. 6.   † 2 Cor. xii. 4, 7.

" The root of bitterness " is there, though it may be out of sight and kept from budding.

It was not so with the blessed Jesus. Even by natural birth He was born of God. His nature, as well as His walk, was sinless; for " He was conceived by the Holy Ghost." Thus, when, after a trial of centuries, both Burnt-offering and Meat-offering had failed in man's hand, Jesus in " the body prepared for Him" came to do His Father's will. These offerings in type shew us how He did it. And He was accepted for us.

(3.) But it is time that we pass on to consider the third particular in which the Meat-offering stood in contrast to the other offerings.

The Meat-offering was *not wholly burnt.** In this it differed from the Burnt-offering. Christ as performing man's duty to God,—that is, the Burnt-offering,—was wholly the food of God, wholly put upon His altar, wholly consumed by Him. But Christ as performing His duty to man,—that is, the Meat-offering,—is also man's meat, the food of the priests :—" The remnant of the meat-offering shall be Aaron's and his sons'; it is a thing most holy of the offerings of the Lord made by fire." Yet even here He satisfies God. " A handful, the memorial of the offering," is put upon the altar, to teach us, that even in fulfilling man's duty to his neighbour, Christ fulfilled it as " an offering unto the Lord."

But though God had thus a portion in the Meat-offering, it is nevertheless specially the food of man;

* Verses 2, 3.

primarily to be viewed as offered *for us* to God, but
also as given *to us*, as priests, to feed on. *For us*, as
Meat-offering, Jesus fulfilled what was due to man.
He did this as our representative, as the substitute of
those who trust Him :—in this aspect of the offering
our souls find peace; here is our acceptance :—but
this, though securing peace, is but a part of our blessed
portion. If Jesus did all this *for us*, will He not do
it *to us ?* As righteous in Him, we still have wants,
we need daily food and anointing; and for these as
much as for righteousness, we are debtors to His
abounding grace. We need Him, and we have Him
as our brother to fulfil His part of the law to us, "for
He came not to destroy, but to fulfil." * The law is,
that the priests should be fed of the altar; they may
not work for their bread as others. The faithful
Israelite is the appointed channel of their subsist-
ence : on his faithfulness, under God, do they depend
for their food. Jesus, as the faithful Israelite, will not
fail the priests who wait at the altar. Let His priests
("ye are a royal priesthood," †) be but found where
they should be, and His offering will be there to feed
them. "He will abundantly bless the provision, He
will satisfy His poor with bread." ‡

We do not sufficiently think of Jesus in this aspect,
as presenting Himself to God as man's meat. The
Gospels, however, are full of it : it shines out in every
page. Jesus, with all His devotedness to God, was
still ever the devoted servant of all around Him. Who

---

* Matt. v. 17.   † 1 Pet. ii. 9.   ‡ Ps. cxxxii. 15.

ever drew upon His love or power, and went away without being satisfied? He opened His hand wide unto His brother, to the poor and the needy in the land. What sorrow was there, what need, what trial, to which Jesus refused to minister?

How precious, then, is Jesus, viewed as Meat-offering! We often want one to fulfil toward us those acts of love and sympathy which our lonely hearts yearn after. Around us there is a heartless world, or brethren, it may be, who can neither sympathise with, nor help us. We think, perhaps, if Jesus were here on earth, we would go to Him and tell Him our sorrows. We are sure, if He were still "the man of sorrows," that we should have a claim on His loving heart. But is He not the same now as in His humili-ation, "the same yesterday, to-day, and for ever?"* Surely He is the same to those who come to Him. Oh, may we learn thus to use Him, that He may satisfy us in every difficulty; when poor to give us bread, when mourning to dry our tears! Weary pilgrim, Jesus is the Meat-offering, to meet *your* claim as well as *God's*. You have a claim on Him; it is your necessity. He must, as a brother, answer it. Come to Him, then, as the One to feed you: it is more blessed for Him to give than for you to receive. Know Him as the One who, when all else fail, has a Meat-offering already provided to satisfy you.

I said that the Meat-offering was *not all burnt;* but though not all burnt, *all was consumed.* In this

* Heb. xiii. 8.

offering the offerer had nothing for himself. God and His priests had the whole between them. How simple, how instructive the lesson! If we could fulfil every duty to God and man according to the standard God has given,—if our bodies were really a living sacrifice, —if we were offered on the sacrifice and service of faith, as Jesus set us an example, what should we have left for self? Just what was left of the Burnt and Meat-offering;—nothing. Between God and man all would be consumed. A holy God and a needy world would require everything.

I would that they, who think to earn heaven by their fulfilment of the law, might learn here what fulfilling the law comes to, and how far it is above and beyond them! The Burnt-offering and the Meat-offering together are God's standard of full obedience : and what a picture do they give us ! The first, the Burnt-offering, requiring perfectness in every member, and then the entire surrender of every member ; the head, the inwards, the legs, all yielded up upon the altar. The next, the Meat-offering, though giving another aspect of devotedness, not a whit behind the Burnt-offering in entire self-surrender ; witness the bruised corn, the oil, the frankincense, and the salt to savour it all. This is God's measure of devotedness ; that is what satisfies Him. One, and but one, has thus satisfied Him ; and in Him, and in Him alone, we may rejoice.

(4.) The fourth point I notice in the Meat-offering is, that, *though intended for, and for the most part consumed by, man, it was, nevertheless, "offered unto*

*the Lord."** In this particular, as in every other, the
Meat-offering has something well worth our notice.
In the Meat-offering the offerer gives himself as
man's meat; yet this is yielded as "an offering unto
Jehovah." The offering indeed fed the priests; but
it was offered, not to them, but to the Lord. The
first Adam took for man not only what was given
him, but what God had reserved for Himself. The
second Adam gave to God not only God's portion, but
even of man's part God had the first memorial. Jesus
as man, in satisfying man's claim on Him, did it as
"an offering unto the Lord."

With us how much even of our graces is offered to
man rather than to God. Even in our most devoted
service, what a seeking there is, perhaps unconsciously,
to be something in the estimation of others: some
secret desire, some undetected wish, even by our very
service to be greater here. The very gifts of God and
the power of His Spirit are sought the better to give
us a place in this world. Thus are our very graces
used to obtain for us glory, not of God, but of those
around us. Surely this is one of the reasons why God
can trust us with so little, for with His gifts we build
up our own name, instead of His name. But how
unlike all this to our Master; yea, how unlike even to
His apostles! "Neither of men," says Paul, "sought
we glory, neither of you, nor yet of others."† This is
our calling, not only to be nothing in the world, but to
be willing to be nothing even among our brethren; to

* Verse 1.   † 1 Thess. ii. 16.

take the nearest place to Him who has indeed taken the lowest.

And in these last days, when through abounding iniquity the love of many is waxing cold,—when the service which the time demands is the only service the Church will not accept,—Christ's example, as here seen in the Meat-offering, is one most precious to us. His service to His neighbour was always "*an offering unto the Lord.*" Thus He gladly was spent for others, though the more He loved them, the less He was loved. May we be thus like Him, that so through grace we may be steadfast. If, on the other hand, our labour of love is offered for man's acceptance, when man rejects us our labour will cease. And surely this is the secret of much of our half-hearted service. But let us when ministering to others, offer ourselves, like Jesus, "unto the Lord," and not unto man ; then, though our love is here slighted, it will be accepted by Him to whom we offer it.

We have thus marked four particulars in which the Meat-offering differed from the other offerings. First, it was of a sweet savour; here it differed from the Sin and Trespass-offerings. Next, it was fed upon by the priests ; here, as well as in its materials, it differed from the Burnt-offering. Then again it left nothing for the offerer ; here it differed from the Peace-offering. It now remains for me to point out,

(5.) In the last place, the contrast between the Meat-offering and *the offering of first-fruits at Pentecost.* The distinction is stated in the twelfth verse :—"As for the oblation of the first-fruits, ye shall offer them unto the Lord, but they shall not be burnt on the altar for a sweet savour." The contrast is this:—the Meat-offering was a sweet savour: the oblation of first-fruits, though very like the Meat-offering, was not so. For the key to this we must turn to Leviticus xxiii., where the law respecting "the oblation of first-fruits" is given to us. In that chapter we have a list of the Feasts. First in order comes the Passover, on the fourteenth day at even :* then the wave-sheaf of first-fruits, on the morrow after the sabbath :† and then, fifty days after, the oblation of the first-fruits on the day of Pentecost.‡ The "*sheaf* of *first-fruits*," on the morrow after the sabbath, might be burnt to the Lord as a sweet savour ;§ but "*the oblation* of the *first-fruits*" at Pentecost might not be burnt on the altar.|| The reason for this distinction is found in the fact, that "*the sheaf* of first-fruits" was unleavened, while "*the oblation* of first-fruits" at Pentecost was mixed and made with leaven.¶

The typical application of all this is too obvious to need any comment. Christ, our Passover, was sacrificed for us, and sacrificed on the predetermined day.** Then "on the morrow after the sabbath," the next ensuing sabbath, that is, on the appointed "first day of the week,"†† Christ "rose from the dead, and became

---

* Chapter xxiii. 5.
‡ Chapter xxiii. 15–17.
|| Chapter ii. 12.
** John xviii. 28; 1 Cor. v. 7.

† Chapter xxiii. 11.
§ Chapter ii. 14–16.
¶ Chapter xxiii. 17.
†† Mark xvi. 1, 2.

the first-fruits of them that slept." * In Him there
was no sin, no leaven ; He was in Himself a sweet
savour to Jehovah. With this offering, therefore, no
Sin-offering was coupled ; it was offered only with a
Burnt-offering and Meat-offering. † But fifty days
after this, " when the day of Pentecost was fully
come," the Church, typified by the leavened oblation
of first-fruits, is offered unto the Lord : for we, as well
as Jesus, are first-fruits ; " we are," says James, " a
kind of *first-fruits* of His creatures." ‡ But this offering, having sin in it, being " mixed with leaven," could
neither stand the test of the fire of the altar, nor be an
offering made by fire of a sweet savour unto the Lord.
Yet it was to be both offered and accepted :—" Ye
shall offer it, but it shall not be burnt." § And why,
and how, was this leavened cake accepted ? Something
was offered " *with it*," for the sake of which the leavened
first-fruits were accepted. They offered with the
leavened bread a Burnt-offering, a Meat-offering, a
Peace-offering, and a Sin-offering ; ‖ for leaven being
found in the oblation of first-fruits, a Sin-offering was
needed with it. And the priest waved *all together :*
" the priest shall wave *them with the bread of the first-
fruits* for a wave-offering before the Lord." The
Church comes with Christ before God ; it is offered
with all the value of His work attached to it. In
itself it cannot stand the trial of God's holiness, for
no measure of oil can naturalise the leaven ; but in

* 1 Cor. xv. 20. † Chapter xxiii. 12, 13. ‡ James i. 18.
§ Chapter ii. 12. ‖ Chapter xxiii. 18, 19.

Christ, and with Christ, and for Christ, it is accepted even as He is. Thus when the Church is presented to God, it comes not alone into His presence, but with the sweet savour of all that Christ has been for it, and with the witness that He has met its sin.

It may be asked, perhaps, why the offering of the Church is represented by a Meat-offering, seeing this offering has such special reference to the second table of the Decalogue? I answer, the Church is not always seen as a Meat-offering. It is *on Pentecost* that it appears in this aspect. There are in the law many types of the Church. She is seen as daughter in the father's house, as wife in the husband's;* and further, she shares with Christ in many of His relations, as offering, as priest, as prophet, or as candlestick. But on Pentecost she is specially seen as a Meat-offering, that is, as man's portion, in active service towards a lost and needy world; because on that day she first stood forth in such service toward man, as taking her part with Christ in loving service to the sons of Adam. Then, "Parthians, and Medes, and Elamites, strangers from Rome, Jews, Proselytes, Cretes, and Arabians," were fed by the service of those, who, though leavened, were yet an appointed and accepted Meat-offering.

Such is the general character of the Meat-offering, as collected from the points in which it differs from the other offerings. I proceed now very briefly to examine it,

II. IN ITS DIFFERENT GRADES OR VARIETIES. These

* Numb. xxx.

are three in number, and represent (as we have already seen,) the different measures of apprehension with which a saint may see Jesus in any of His relations. The first class or grade is *unbaked flour;** this is the most perfect type of the Meat-offering: the second is *baked loaves* or *cakes;* † in this emblem one or two particulars are lost sight of: the third, *green ears dried by the fire,* ‡ is lower still than either of the others. Each gives us Jesus as Meat-offering, that is, as meeting and fulfilling man's claim on Him: in all He is equally "a sweet savour," § in all equally acceptable to God: but the second class gives a higher view of His perfectness in this relation than the third; and again the first class is higher than either. The first class shews us an offering like that of the princes; ‖ the next gives us something lower; ¶ the last class shews us the offering in its rudest form, "ears of corn dried by the fire." The Lord lead us to see Jesus more fully, according to the measure of the first class, that our joy and strength may increase. We must rejoice in proportion as we see His perfectness; for His offering is all ours; it was "offered *for* us."

Observe, then, the chief distinctions between the different grades of the Meat-offering.

(1.) The first contrast is, that while *in the first grade*

---

* Verse 1.   † Verses 4–7.   ‡ Verse 14.   § Verses 2, 9, 12, 16.
‖ Compare verse 1, and Numb. vii. 13, 19, 25, &c.

¶ Here, too, there is within this class a measure of variety, as the Meat-offering baked in the oven and in the pan. The difference, however, I believe, is merely connected with *the size* of the offering. A large loaf could not be baked in a frying-pan.

*each article of the materials is enumerated,** *the second describes the offering more generally as* "*unleavened wafers anointed.*"† The import of this distinction is at once and easily discoverable. How many saints are there, who, in thinking or speaking about Jesus, can fully assert that He is "*unleavened,*" who know and believe He is sinless, while yet they cannot see all His perfectness. But absence of evil, the being without leaven, is a lower thought than the possession of perfect goodness. We can say, "He did no sin, neither was guile found in His mouth," long before we can tell what was in Him, and the way in which He spent it all for others.

(2.) A second point of contrast between the different grades of the Meat-offering is too remarkable to be omitted. *In the first class it is observed, that the offerer himself takes the memorial for God out of the offering :*‡ *in the second, the priest is said to take it :*§ while in the last class,—"in the dried ears,"—no mention is made who takes it. ‖ We observed a distinction similar to this in the Burnt-offering : in the first class the offerer killed the victim ; in the last, the priest did. The difference is obvious and instructive. The one view shews Christ *in His person* as offerer ; the other *in His appointed office* as the priest. The first, Christ as offerer personally giving to God, is a higher view than Christ offering as priest officially. The latter view loses, at least, one precious

---

* Verses 1, 2.   † Verse 4.   ‡ Verse 2.
§ Verse 9.   ‖ Verse 16.

object in the precious offering of Jesus: the office is indeed seen, but the person of the Lord quite lost sight of.

(3.) But there is a third contrast, and one which may be more generally apprehended, between the first class of the Meat-offering and the others. *In the first class Christ's offering is seen as flour: He is "the fine flour" bruised. In the other classes this particular is almost merged: He is rather bread, either "loaves" or "wafers."* * The distinction here is very manifest. We may see Jesus as our "*bread*," or even as God's bread, without entering into the thoughts which are suggested by the emblems of "*fine flour*" and "*frankincense.*" The perfect absence of all unevenness, and the deep bruisings which He endured that He might satisfy us; the precious savour also of the offering, only more fragrant when tried by fire; these are not our first views of Jesus: for as they are the most perfect apprehensions, so are they generally the last.

(4.) The difference between the first class of the Meat-offering and the third is even more striking and manifest: *this latter offering giving us a thought of Christ as "first-fruits,"* the first sheaf of the ripening harvest, *rather than the bread already prepared for food, or the fine flour as seen in the first grade.*† This distinction I need not dwell upon, as its general bearing is sufficiently clear. Suffice it to say, that here, as in the latter grades of the other offerings, we lose

---

* Compare verses 1 and 4.   † Compare verses 1 and 14.

what is distinctive or peculiar in the particular offering, while a thought or view of some other offering is in measure substituted in its place. We have already seen this to be the case in the Burnt-offering: we shall find it again in the Sin-offerings. The fact is, that these classes are measures of apprehension. When the measure of apprehension is small, one view of the offering is confounded with another view. The building, to repeat a former illustration, is seen too indistinctly to observe its different aspects: more than one side of it is seen at once, though neither of these sides is seen very distinctly. This, I doubt not, is the case here. The thought of the Meat-offering is joined with that of the First-fruits. How many true Christians are there whose views of Christ are thus without definiteness; Sin-offering, Meat-offering, Burnt-offering, all mixed together.

Such are some of the Varieties in this Offering; and if they teach no more, they teach us at least what Christians lose from their lack of knowledge: for many a precious truth seen in the first grade, is in the lower grades wholly overlooked. For instance, in the first grade, all the materials are seen, "the flour, the oil, the salt, the frankincense;" while nearly the whole of this is lost in the lower grades, where it is only noticed that the offering is "unleavened." Is it to be supposed that this mere negative knowledge, this bare knowledge of what Christ was not, can ever have the same effect upon our souls as the full apprehension of what He really was? So again, in the first grade

Christ's person is seen: the offerer is seen himself offering. Need we be told how different is the effect of merely seeing Christ's office in His atonement? And so of the rest. He who, seeing the first-fruits, confounds or substitutes this thought for that of the Meat-offering, though he sees Christ, does not see Him as fulfilling the Law, but simply as the first sheaf of a promised harvest. There are many who believe that Christ is risen as the first-fruits of them that slept, who by no means see how, by His offering for them, they also are accepted in Him. But I will not pursue the subject. Such as have intelligence will be able to trace it for themselves. Others, I fear, would scarce understand the mere outline, which is all that I could here give of it.

Here I close my remarks on the Meat-offering. More, much more, might be said. What has been said, I trust, may, through grace, lead us, first to bless God for having given us such an offering; and then to desire a greater insight into all that Jesus has been for us. For ever blessed be our God who has thus loved us. May we daily know more of His love.

G

THE PEACE-OFFERING.

LEVITICUS III., AND VII. 11–21 AND 29–34.

WE now come to the sacrifice of PEACE-OFFERINGS, the last offered of all the typical offerings. Accordingly, we shall find it revealing to us that aspect of Christ's offering, which is generally the last apprehended by the believer. And I may add, that as it was 'burnt upon the Burnt-offering,"* and was directly consequent upon it, so it reveals to us the consequences of those aspects of Christ's offering which are prefigured in the Burnt and Meat-offerings.

We may examine it, first, *in its contrasts to the other offerings,* that is, as bringing out one definite and particular aspect of Christ's offering; and then, secondly, in *its several varieties,* as shewing the different apprehensions enjoyed by Christians of this aspect.

I. And, first, IN ITS CONTRAST TO THE OTHER OFFER-INGS, it may be sufficient to enumerate two chief points: (1.) It was a sweet-savour offering; and, (2.) The offerer, God, and the priest were fed by it. In the former of these particulars, it differed from the Sin-offerings; in the latter, it differed from all others.

* See chapter iii. 5.

(1.) *It was a "sweet-savour" offering.** On the import of this distinction, I need here say little, since we have already more than once examined it. Suffice it to say that here, as in the Burnt and Meat-offerings, we are presented with a view of the offering, not as offered with any reference to sin, but rather as shewing man giving to God that which is sweet and pleasant to Him.

But the Burnt-offering and Meat-offering were both "sweet savours." This particular, therefore, though distinguishing the Peace-offering from the Sin-offerings, gives us nothing by which we may distinguish it from the other sweet-savour offerings. I pass on, therefore, to the next particular, in which the Peace-offering very distinctly differs from the Burnt and Meat-offerings.

(2.) The second point in which the Peace-offering differed from others was, that *in it the offerer, the priest, and God, all fed together*. This was the case in no offering but the Peace-offering. In this they had something in common. Here each had a part. They held communion in feeding on the same offering.

We have first *the offerer's part;* then *God's part;* then *the priest's part;* and included in this last, though separately mentioned, *the part which was fed upon by the priest's children.*†

And what a view does this give of the efficacy of the offering! how does it magnify "the unsearchable

* Verses 5, 16.
† See chapter vii. 31, 32, and compare Numbers xviii. 9-11.

riches of Christ!" God, man, and the priest, all fed together, all finding satisfaction in the offering. *God* first has His part and is satisfied, for He declares it to be very good. "It is an offering made by fire of a sweet savour unto the Lord."* *Man* (in Christ) as offerer has his part, and is permitted to share this offering with his friends.† And *the priest*, that is, Christ in His official character, is satisfied also, and *His children* are satisfied with Him.‡ What a picture is here presented to us! The offerer feasts with God, with His priest, and with the priest's children.

[i.] In the Peace-offering *the offerer feasts*, in other words, finds satisfaction, and feeds upon the same offering of which a part has already satisfied God: for a part of the Peace-offering, (as we shall see in the sequel,) "the fat, the blood, the inwards," before the offerer can touch his part, must have already been consumed on the altar.

We get nothing like this either in the Burnt or Meat-offering. In them we have *the offering satisfying God;* all consumed by His fire, and ascending to Him, as in the Burnt-offering; or shared, as in the Meat-offering, with His priests. But in all this, though God was satisfied, the offerer got no part of the offering. The Burnt and Meat-offerings were (as we have already seen) the emblem of the perfect fulfilment of the law's requirements. In them we see man (in Christ) offering to God that which perfectly satisfies Him. God finds food in the offering, and declares it to be very good.

* Chapter iii. 5.   † Chapter vii. 16.   ‡ Chapter vii. 31.

But in all this the offerer has nothing. The Peace-offering shews us *the offerer himself satisfied.*

Now the offerer here, as elsewhere, is Christ; Christ in His person standing *"for us."** But the extent to which we are interested in this, and the fact that, till we realize it, the Peace-offering is unintelligible, require that I should dwell here for a moment, before I proceed to details.

I repeat, then, that in all the offerings, Christ, as offerer, stands as our representative. Whether it be in the Sin-offering, the Burnt-offering, the Meat-offering, or the Peace-offering, He is the man Christ Jesus *"for us."* He is *for us* without the camp, *for us* put upon the altar, *for us* bearing our sins, *for us* accepted and satisfied. And when we say He did this *"for us,"* we mean that He did it *instead of us,* nay, *as us.* Thus, when He was judged, He was judged as us. When He kept the law, He kept it as us. When He was accepted, He was accepted as us; and so when He was satisfied, He was satisfied as us.

Now, the consequence of Christ's thus standing "for us" is, that what is true of Him, is true of all who are in Him. Thus the offerings, in shewing us Christ's position, in shewing Him, only shew us our own; nay, I may say, when they shew us Christ, they shew us the Church, for He stood "for us." "As He is, so are we in this world:" † we are "accepted in the Beloved."‡ I do not say that this is apprehended even by those who are seen of God to stand in these blessings. I

* Eph. v. 2.　　　† 1 John iv. 17.　　　‡ Eph. i. 6.

need not say how little "we apprehend of that for which we are apprehended." * I simply state the fact, that in all those relations which are typified by the various offerings, Jesus in offering them as a man stood "for us;" He stood *as us;* nay, *He was us,* if I may say so. When Christ offered, God saw us offering; for Christ stood as offerer "for us." God looked upon Christ *as us.* He sees us, therefore, *as Christ* before Him.† And just as truly as Christ stood for us and as us, so as a consequence do we stand in Him to God-ward. What He did, we are reckoned to have done, for as us He did it. So what He enjoys, we enjoy, for as us He enjoys it.

Now this last thought is the thought of the Peace-offering. Christ is satisfied and fed by His offering. But in this He stands for us; and therefore we are satisfied as soon as we thus apprehend Him. The thought may be a little more complex than that of the Sin and Burnt-offering; but it proceeds exactly on the same principle. Just as the feeble believer in Christ, when he sees Christ offering the Sin-offering, sees that God's wrath against sin has been met, for Jesus standing instead of us as man has borne it;—just as the same feeble saint, when He sees Christ offering the Burnt and Meat-offering, sees that God and His requirements have been satisfied, for Jesus standing for us as man has satisfied them;—just so the same believer when he sees Christ offering the Peace-offering, sees that man is satisfied with the offering, for

* Phil. iii. 12.   † See 1 Cor. xii. 12; "So also is Christ."

Jesus standing for us as man is satisfied. And as our sense of acceptance depends on realizing Him as accepted for us, so our sense of satisfaction and communion with God depends on realizing Him in communion for us. Thus seeing the Peace-offering, and by it finding that Christ as man is satisfied, is to those who know themselves " in Christ," to find that they themselves are satisfied.

I fear that there are but too many saints who never realize this aspect of the Offering, and therefore never fully experience that satisfaction which the Offering has purchased for them. I do not say that the blessing is not theirs ; this and all else is theirs, if they are " *in Christ.*" But those things which are true for them in Him, are not realized by them in their own experience. Experience is, I again repeat, nothing more than our measure of apprehension of that which is already true for us in Christ. Thank God, the sufficiency of His work does not depend upon our apprehension of it. But our satisfaction depends much on our apprehension. It is because we apprehend so little that we have so little comfort.

And our strength particularly depends on our apprehension of that view of Christ which the Peace-offering teaches ; for strength is sustained by food, and the Peace-offering shews man fed by the sacrifice. Yet how little is this view of Christ apprehended ! Am I asked the cause? It is because so few really know acceptance. As long as it is at all a question with you whether God has accepted you or not, your chief desire will be to know *God satisfied*, far rather than to be *satisfied yourself*. As a criminal whose reprieve has not yet come, you will not ask, Have I bread for to-day? but, Am I pardoned? Death stares you in the face: you cannot think of food or raiment. But let the question of acceptance be settled: let this be fully known; and then you will find time to listen to the cravings of that new nature, which needs to be sustained and nourished. What is to satisfy this? Nothing but the precious meat of the altar. And this is shewn as provided for us in Jesus, when we see Him, as our representative, the offerer of the Peace-offering.

And here observe *what the offerer feasts on.* He feasts on the meat of the altar: his food is the spotless offering which has already satisfied the Lord.

Now this offering represents "the body of Jesus,"* including His walk, His thoughts, His strength, His affections. These, as we saw in the Burnt-offering, were the things He sacrificed; and because they were unblemished, they were accepted. As a sweet savour they satisfied God. But they give satisfaction, too, because they are unblemished, to the offerer. Christ finds His meat in His own offering. He "is satisfied with the travail of His soul."†

Jesus as offerer stands "for us;" and by His feeding on the offering, He shews how man is satisfied. Would to God His people might learn here what, as respects atonement, will alone satisfy them. Out of God's presence man seeks food in many things. He may try

* Heb. x. 5–10.   † Isa. liii. 11.

"the riotous living of the far country:" yea, in his hour of need he may come to "the husks which the swine eat."* In seeking God's presence too, not a few have yet to learn what alone can give peace and satisfaction in that presence. Some of those who are longing to feast with God, are seeking satisfaction in their frames or feelings. Others are trying their own righteousness, their experiences, their walk, their service. Are these things the unblemished meat of the altar? Is it by these things Christ has satisfied God? Are our experiences, our frames, our feelings, the things on which, as respects atonement, Christ and God have fellowship? If not, they cannot be the meat upon which we, as needing atonement, are to feed with God. If Christ as man could not have communion with God through anything save a spotless offering, so neither can any of His members: if they are fed at all, they must be fed as He is. Oh, let us be wise and see our calling, nor seek satisfaction save in Jesus! He is the only perfect One; out of Him there is nothing fit for the altar, nothing suited therefore to feed our souls. When Christ feeds with God on that which is blemished; when He makes a Peace-offering of the unclean; then, nor till then, let us seek our food in the unclean, the torn, the blemished. But while we see that even He, as far as atonement is concerned, can only be fed with His own perfect unblemished offering, let us as in Him reject all others, and feed and be satisfied in Him.

How important is the lesson taught here; how unan-

* Luke xv. 13, 15, 16.

swerably does it express this truth, that, as respects atonement at least, the Christian has nothing to feed on with God, but that which Christ Himself feeds on with Him: that however right our experiences or attainments or walk or service may be in their place, they are not the offering for atonement, nor can they ever be the ground of peace. And indeed, for a Christian to seek his food in these things, is as though an Israelite were to take his garments to feed on. In truth the man who seeks satisfaction in his own attainments just does this: what should be his raiment, he makes his meat. The garments of the Israelite are the appointed symbol of a man's deportment and manifested character.* So the New Testament interprets the type: "The fine linen is the righteousness of saints."† This garment might be easily defiled. But let us suppose it clean: are garments to be fed on? The type answers at once: it is the meat of the altar, the sweet savour alone, which satisfies. Our prayers, our love, our service, these things, like the leavened cake at Pentecost,‡ though accepted for the sake of what accompanies them, are one and all in themselves blemished. In one sense indeed, our services are a "sweet savour;"§ but it is only in the same sense that our persons are "righteous." In either case the works and persons are accounted to be what in themselves they are not, in virtue of that perfect Work and Person, in whom

* Psalm lxxiii. 6, cix. 18; Isa. lii. 1, lix. 17, lxi. 3; Zech. iii. 3; Col. iii. 8, 12; Rev. iii. 4, xvi. 15, &c.
† Rev. xix. 8.   ‡ See page 91.   § Phil. iv. 18.

and through whom they are offered. Just as the sinner, though in himself vile, is accounted righteous in Him through whom we have received the atonement; so are His offerings, though leavened, accounted sweet in the savour of that through which they are offered. The sinner accepted in Christ becomes indeed himself, in spirit, both an offerer and offering; yet even then his "spiritual sacrifices," whether of work or worship, are only "acceptable to God by Jesus Christ."* Like "the leavened cake" already referred to, our works or worship, because imperfect, could never be accepted, did they not come before God with the sweet savour, and as the consequence of another and a perfect offering. Were they offered to make atonement they would be rejected. They are only accepted because atonement has been already made. To make atonement, there must be perfection in the offering: God will not be satisfied with ought less than a perfect sacrifice. If we wish to be fed and satisfied with Him, it must be in and through that "One offering" which has already satisfied His holiness.

But this leads us to the next particular in the Peace-offering; namely, that,

[ii.] *The offerer feasts with God.* Man (in Christ) and God find common food. The offering is shared between them. The thought here is not, as in the Burnt-offering, merely that God finds satisfaction in the offering. It includes this, but it goes further. It shews communion; for God and man share together.

* 1 Pet. ii. 5.

I would that this aspect of the Offering were more familiar to the minds of Christians: how would it raise their thoughts of the value of the Offering, and of the place, which, through the Offering, man is called to! We should not, we could not, truly realize the joy and satisfaction God finds in the Offering, without obtaining more exalted views of its wondrous preciousness and efficacy. We could not behold man sharing with God in that which God declares to be most precious to Him, without being led to a far deeper apprehension of man's high and blessed destiny. But are these our thoughts of the Offering? Do we, when we think of it, think of the joy God finds in it; or do we thus habitually realize the place into which it puts man as sharer with God? Alas! to how many are such thoughts strangers; and the reason is, because as yet they have not seen the Peace-offering. If only they may be delivered from wrath! If only they may hope for acceptance! This is all many saints hope for, this is practically all they expect. But is this all that the Offering has purchased? Is this all that Christ enjoys? Is His place bare acceptance? Is His portion only pardon? Is He not, as man, God's heir and first-born, the One in whom His soul delights, the One with whom God holds unbroken fellowship, to whom He reveals all His mind? And does Jesus hold this alone? Are we not, in Him, called to the same communion? Are we not in all,—His fellow-heirs, His joy, His bride, His members? The Peace-offering answers the question when it shews us man feasting with Jehovah; when it tells us that

Christ's place is our place, and that in Him we are called to share with God.

And how clearly does this portion of the type give the answer to the question, What is communion? Communion is simply sharing; to have communion, therefore, we must have something to share; and to have communion with a holy God, we must have something which we can share with Him. We cannot share nothing, and He will not share with us in the unclean. Our attainments, therefore, cannot yield communion, nor our works, for the best have sin in them. But, thank God, there is a perfect offering, the offering of our blessed Lord; and if we would have communion with God, the only way is to share that offering.

And this at once gives us the key to the cause of our general and acknowledged lack of communion. Of intercourse we have enough, perhaps too much. Of communion, how very little! The reason is, so little of Christ's Offering is apprehended, that when believers meet they have scarce anything of Him to share. And the same is true of our approaches to God, for there may be intercourse with God without communion. How often when we approach God do we speak to Him only about our feelings, our experiences, our sins, our trials. All this is right; we cannot be without these, and we are right to tell them to our Father. But after all, this of itself is not communion, nor will speaking of these things ever yield it to us. Let us come before God to be filled with Christ, to be taken up with Him, His life, His ways, His sweetness; let the confession of our failure and nothingness in ourselves be made the plea that we may be filled with Him; and our intercourse will be soon changed to communion, for in Him we shall have something we can share. May the Lord lead us more into His presence, there to be taught what we possess in Jesus; and then, when we meet our brethren or our Father, we shall feast together on what there is in Him.

[iii.] But further, in the sacrifice of Peace-offerings, *the offerer feasts with the priest.** The sacrificing priest, as I have already observed, is always Christ, viewed *in His official character* as Mediator. We learn here how the offering, which He offered as man, feeds, that is, satisfies Him, not only *as man*, but also *as Mediator*.

To understand this we must recollect and apprehend the varied relations in which Christ stands connected with the offering; for He appears for us in many offices, in more than one relation. In connexion with the Offering alone, we see Him, as I have said, in at least three characters. He stands as *offerer*, but He is also *the offering;* and He who is both offerer and offering is also *priest.* Yet each of these is a distinct relation; each gives us a different thought of Christ. As *offerer* He is presented to us *as man:* there is one in our nature satisfying God. Thus in the offerer we rather see Christ's *person:* it is a man standing for men. The *offering* gives us another thought. It is not Himself, so much as *what He did.* Here it is not His

* Chapter vii. 32, 33.

person, so much as *His work and character,* which the type brings before us. The *priest* again is even more distinct. It is Christ in *His office* as Mediator : here it is neither Christ's person nor His work, but *one of His offices,* that is presented to us.

Now, if this simple distinction be apprehended, as I think it must be more or less by every Christian, it will be manifest that there are things true of Christ in one relation which are by no means true of Him in another. For instance, His intercession for us is as priest. As the offering, He does not intercede ; as lamb, He dies for us. So again as priest and offerer, He is fed ; as the lamb, as the offering, He is not fed. Now there are offerings in which the priest finds food, but from participating in which the offerer is excluded : some of the Sin-offerings are of this latter character, for in them the priest is fed, while the offerer has nothing. The Sin-offerings, as we shall see more fully in the sequel, are man *satisfying offended justice.* They are not man giving something sweet to God, but man receiving from God in his offering the penalty of sin. These Sin-offerings supply food to the priest,* that is, Christ *as Mediator* finds satisfaction in them, but they afford Him no food *as man* the offerer : *as man* in them He only confesses sin. The *priest,* God's official servant, is satisfied, because offended justice is vindicated : but *man,* who pays the penalty in his offering, finds no satisfaction in the act.

The Peace-offering gives us a very different view of

* Chapter vi. 25–30.

the offering. In it man, as well as the priest, is satisfied. In bearing the penalty of sin, that is, in the Sin-offering, man found no satisfaction. But he does find it in the sacrifice of Peace-offerings; here he shares the offering with God. Nor is the priest excluded from this offering: the Peace-offering feeds him too. If, as priest, Christ found satisfaction in the Sin-offering, that offering which only vindicated offended justice, we might expect to find Him equally satisfied in the offering which fed both God and man. And the Peace-offering reveals that it is so. God and man feast in peace together; and the Priest, the common friend of both, seeing them satisfied, is Himself satisfied also.

How blessed is the thought here revealed to us! how does it open to us the heart of Christ, the joy which He feels as Mediator in seeing communion instituted between God and man! Surely we lose not a little in our communion, if we forget the joy which the Mediator finds in it; if we overlook the satisfaction which He experiences when He sees man at peace with God. He who knows the full value of the offering, never forgets that by it the priest is fed. And if the presence of beloved friends enhances the sweetness of each earthly blessing; and if the absence of those we love makes the full cup lose half its enjoyment; how much must it enhance our joy to know that He who loves us is feasting with us; what must they lose of the sweetness of communion who forget that in it our Priest is fed! This I know, Christ never forgets that when He feasts, He feasts with us. Even yet He says, as once of old, "With desire I desire to eat this sacrifice with you."* Shall we, then, have no thought of His joy; shall we forget the satisfaction He finds in the offering? Those who can do this have as yet learnt but little of the Peace-offering; for in the Peace-offering the Priest is fed.

[iv.] But the type takes us further still, and shews us *the Priest's children also sharing with the offerer* in the Peace-offering.† They, too, as well as the offerer, the priest, and God, find satisfaction in this blessed offering. Our first question here, of course, must be,—Who are represented by the *Priest's children?*

We have already seen that the Priest is Christ; Christ viewed in His official character as Mediator. His children, that is, His family, are therefore the Church; but the Church viewed in one particular aspect. The Church, like her blessed Lord, stands both to God and man in more than one relation; and each of these different relations requires in the type a different emblem. This we have abundantly seen is true of Christ: but it is no less true of the Church, His body. For instance, just as the varied pictures we have considered,—the offering, the priest, the offerer, —all shew out our blessed Lord, while yet each shews Him in a different character; so in like manner is it with the Church also. She, too, has varied relations, which require varied emblems. In one we see her in

* Luke xxii. 15.
† Chap. vii. 31, 32, compared with Numb. xviii. 9–11.

H

service for God; in another in communion with Him.
Israel, as the chosen nation, represents *the Church as
"the peculiar people,"* looked at simply as the seed of
Abraham, and as such, in covenant with God. The
Levites give us a different thought: they shew us *the
Church in service;* as ministering for God before men,
carrying His ark, and caring for His tabernacle.* The
family of Priests give us yet another thought. Here
we have *the Church in communion with God;* as the
seed of the High Priest and Mediator, sharing with
Him in His access to God and in intercession; having
a right to stand in the holy place, where no eye sees
them but God's.

If this be seen, it will sufficiently reveal the import
of the Priest's children feeding on the Peace-offering.
Their share in the sacrifice shews us the Church in
communion, sharing with the Offerer in the satisfaction
afforded by the Offering. To me this is a blessed
thought, marking the extent and efficacy of this precious
offering. Just as of old he that really feasted with God
in the Peace-offering, could not do so without sharing
with God's priests; so now communion with God, if
enjoyed at all, must be shared with all in communion
with Him. This is no question of choice: it cannot be

* I may observe here that both Priests and Levites are types of
the whole Church, not of a part of it. We are told that by God's express command " the Levites were not numbered among the children of Israel." (Numbers i. 47, 54, and ii. 33.) By this appointment the tribe of Levi was purposely separated, so that it might
not be looked at merely as a part of Israel. Thus it constitutes a
distinct picture, and shews a distinct relation of the Church.

otherwise ; for he that is in communion with God must
be in communion also with all whom He communes
with. We may indeed be accepted in the Beloved,
while yet we do not know our calling, or the relation-
ship which exists in Christ between us and all His
redeemed worshippers. But it is impossible to realize
our standing in Christ, as offerers and partakers in Him
of the Peace-offering, without finding that the Offering
in which we rejoice links us with the joy of all God's
spiritual priesthood.

And here let me observe in connexion with this
particular, that it is possible for believers to find satisfaction in the offering *as priest's children,* when through
ignorance of their union with Christ as the Offerer,
they find no satisfaction *as offerers* in Him of the
Peace-offering. Alas! the great mass of God's Israel
are captives in Babylon or Egypt; cut off, though born
to it, from the exercise of priesthood and sacrifice, and
from the sacred meat of the altar. But even of those
who do know the power of redemption, and who have
fed on the offerings of the Lord, how few know that meat
save as priests; how few apprehend it as offerers of the
Peace-offering! I would that all saints fed as priest's
children, but not less that they fed as offerers in Christ.
To find satisfaction *as priest's children* in the offering,
we need not know our oneness with Christ as Offerer.
It is enough to see that He as the faithful Israelite has
offered, and that we as priest's children have a claim on
the sacrifice. But this measure of apprehension will
not suffice to make us realize our share in the Peace-

offering *as offerers*. To know that Christ as Offerer
has offered, will not give us the food which belongs to
the offerer, unless we apprehend our oneness with Him,
that He stood for us, that we are "in Him." This,
alas! how few now see: how few therefore take the
offerer's part in the Peace-offering. Thank God, if we
know our priesthood, this relation alone will provide us
meat: for another has satisfied God, and His priests
may feed with Him. But while we do this, and rejoice
in this relation, may the Lord lead us on to see yet
another,—that our place is also "in Christ" as Offerer,
and that we have satisfied God in Him. This as much
as priesthood is our calling. May we but apprehend
what we are apprehended for!

There is a particular connected with participation
in the Peace-offering, which is incidentally mentioned
here, and which we must not overlook; namely, that
*none, even though of the Priest's family, could eat of
the offering unless they were clean.* There is a difference between being a priest and being clean. The
fact of a man's contracting some defilement did not
prove him to be no priest. On the contrary, the rules
respecting clean and unclean were only for God's elect.
This is very important truth. May the Lord make us
all understand it better. It teaches us that it is one
thing to be a priest; another thing to be a clean priest;
yet the unclean priest, if of the chosen seed, is still in
the covenant, and on very different ground from the
seed of strangers. The Israelite, who through contact

* Chapter vii. 20.

with uncleanness, might for a while be excluded from
the Tabernacle, could at any time be restored again by
using the appointed washings. Still his uncleanness
for the time made him as a stranger, and cut him off
from the meat of God.

The details of the law on this point* are well
worthy our deepest attention. We learn that "leprosy"
or "the running issue" excluded even a son of Aaron
from the camp; the period of his exclusion depending
on the time during which the disease was manifest.
"Leprosy" and "the running issue" were both breakings out of the flesh, breakings out which were manifest
to others, though manifested differently. They typify
those outbreaks of the flesh in the Christian, which
are too flagrant to be hid from others. The appointed
discipline for these, now as of old, is temporary exclusion from the camp.† During this period the priest's
child was still a priest; but to little purpose, for he
was cut off from the altar. But there were defilements
of a less manifest character than leprosy, less discernible
by the eyes of man, which yet brought with them
temporary uncleanness, and with it temporary exclusion
from the Tabernacle. If a child of the priest touched
any dead thing, or anything which was unclean by
contact with the dead; or if he touched any creeping
thing whereby he might be made unclean, or a man of
whom he might take uncleanness, the law was express,
—"The soul that hath touched any such shall be
unclean until the even, and shall not eat of the holy

* See Leviticus xxii. 1–7.   † 1 Cor. v. 13.

things unless he wash his flesh with water." A spiritual priest may in like manner contract defilement, and so have his communion hindered. If our spirits (for this dispensation is spiritual, not carnal,) come in contact with the spirit of the world, if its dead things are felt to touch us, if its creeping things affect our souls, no visible impression may be left to be seen by others, while yet we ourselves may feel our communion hindered. At such a time we may not, under a penalty of judgment,* approach that which at other times is our food. Thank God, contact with the unclean, though it hinders our sense of communion, cannot remove the blood of the covenant. That still remains before God. We may not see it perhaps; He always sees it. Yet who would willingly be the unclean priest, cut off from participation with the altar; his days lost to God and to His tabernacle; his food eaten in the dark?†

Such are the chief particulars in which the Peace-offering differed from the other offerings. It was the sweet-savour offering in which not only God was satisfied, but in which man and the priest found satisfaction also.

I now pass on to observe,

II. THE DIFFERENT GRADES OR VARIETIES WHICH ARE OBSERVED IN THIS OFFERING. These shew us the different measures of intelligence with which this view of Christ's offering may be apprehended.

And here, as there are several distinct sharers in the

---

* Compare Lev. vii. 20, 21, and 1 Cor. xi. 29.

† He might not eat it until after sunset. See Lev. xxii. 7.

offering,—for God, man, and the Priest, have each a portion,—it may be well to consider each portion separately with its particular differences, since in each portion there are distinct varieties observed.

(1.) First, then, as to *God's part* in the Peace-offering. In this certain varieties at once present themselves; some of them relating to the value of the offering, others connected with the offerer's purport in the oblation.

[i.] To speak first of *the varieties touching the value of the offering.* We have here, just as in the Burnt-offering, *several different grades.* There is the "bullock," "the lamb," "the goat;" and these respectively represent here what they do in the Burnt-offering. Each gives us rather a different thought as to the character of Christ's blessed offering. But it is to be noticed here, that although in the Peace-offering we have nearly the same number of grades as in the Burnt-offering, in the details of these various grades we do not find nearly so much difference as is the case in the Burnt-offering. There is, indeed, the variety of "bullock," "lamb," and "goat," shewing that the offering is apprehended under these various characters; but nearly all the rest seen respecting this portion of the offering, as to the mode of the oblation and the part taken by the offerer, is much the same. It will be remembered that, in the different grades of the Burnt-offering, a great variety was observed in the mode of oblation. In some the parts of the victim were seen to be discriminated; in others this was not so: in some a portion of the offering was seen to be washed in water; in others this was overlooked: in some the offerer was seen laying his hand on the offering; in others this was not observed: in some the offerer himself was seen to kill the offering; in others the priest killed it. But in the Peace-offering we lose this great variety, for in each grade the offering is treated nearly alike. There are indeed the different grades, but this is nearly all: and even these grades do not vary here so much as in the Burnt-offering.*

The import of this is sufficiently plain. It teaches that if God's part of the Peace-offering be apprehended at all, it will be apprehended nearly equally. If Christ is seen at all as offering the Peace-offering to God, the view of Him will lack no important particular, nor will His office be confounded with His person, nor will the various parts of His work be overlooked. The difference, for the most part, will simply have reference to the general character of the offering as "goat," "lamb," or "bullock."

[ii.] But there are other varieties noticed in the type, as to that part of the Peace-offering which was offered to God, which are connected, not with the value of the offering, but *with the offerer's purport in bringing the oblation.* If we turn to the seventh chapter, where the distinction I refer to is mentioned, it will be seen that the Peace-offering might be offered in *two* ways. It might be offered either *as a thanksgiving,* that is, for

* The "turtle-dove," that is, the lowest view of the offering, is omitted.

praise ;* or *as a vow or voluntary offering*, that is, for
service.† If it were seen to be offered "*for thanksgiving*," many particulars are noticed respecting man's
share in it, which are entirely lost sight of and omitted
when it is seen to be offered "*for a vow.*" And most
of the varieties in the Peace-offering (I may say *all* the
varieties touching the Priest's and Offerer's part in it)
depend upon the view which may be taken of the
general character of the offering, whether it were
offered "*for thanksgiving*," or whether it were offered
"*for a vow.*" What these particular differences are, we
shall note in their proper order and place when we come
to consider the Varieties in the Priest's and Offerer's
part of the Peace-offering. Suffice it here to state the
import of the general distinction between "the Thanksgiving" and "the Vow;" and to shew wherein the
view of the Peace-offering as seen offered "*for thanksgiving*," differed from the Peace-offering to be offered
"*for a vow.*"

To understand this, we must remember what the
Offering was. It was Christ, as our representative,
giving Himself to God for us. But the purport of this
offering may be very differently apprehended : it may
be seen as offered *for praise*, or *in service*. Jesus
may be seen as offering Himself *for God's glory ;* this
is the offering "*for praise :*" or He may be seen offering Himself *in God's service ;* this is the offering "*for
a vow.*" Most Christians, I believe all of us at first,

* Chapter vii. 12, "for praise." So the LXX., and many versions.
† Chapter vii. 16.

regard Christ's offering rather as *a matter of service*: we look on the atonement as something done by Christ *in God's service;* rather than as something which, from first to last, was *for God's glory.* Of course these two views are most intimately connected ; but I note here, that though connected, they are distinct : and the difference, if it be seen in nothing else, is immediately seen in the results of either. It will be found in the type, and our experience confirms this, that the apprehension of Christ as bringing an offering *for God's glory* will lead us at once to far deeper and more extended views of its consequences, than the view of Christ as offering Himself *in God's service.* Accordingly, when the offering is apprehended as offered "*for praise,*" then many details and consequences connected with it are seen also, which are entirely omitted or lost sight of when the offering is seen as offered "*for a vow.*"*

Having thus briefly marked the varieties in the Peace-offering, in that part which was offered to God, as shewing the different apprehensions which may be entertained by saints of this aspect of Christ's offering, we now proceed to consider,

(2.) *The Priest's and Offerer's part,* and the varieties which are observable here. It will be found that the particulars respecting this portion of the Peace-offering differ very much according as the offering is apprehended "for praise " or "for service." "*If he offer it for a*

---

* Compare verses 12–15, which describe the offering "for praise," with verses 16–18, which describe the offering "for a vow."

thanksgiving (or for praise), then he shall offer with the sacrifice of thanksgiving unleavened cakes mingled with oil, and unleavened wafers anointed with oil, and cakes mingled with oil, of fine flour, fried. Besides the cakes, he shall offer for his offering leavened bread with the sacrifice of thanksgiving of his peace-offerings. And of it he shall offer one out of the whole oblation for an heave-offering unto the Lord, and it shall be the priest's that sprinkleth the blood of the peace-offerings. And the flesh of the sacrifice of his peace-offerings for thanksgiving shall be eaten the same day that it is offered ; he shall not leave any of it until the morning. *But if the sacrifice of his offering be a vow,* or a voluntary offering, it shall be eaten the same day that he offereth his sacrifice : and on the morrow also the remainder of it shall be eaten : but the remainder of the flesh of the sacrifice on the third day shall be burnt with fire."*

Such is the law : let us now note these particulars.

When offered *"for praise,"* [i.] *a Meat-offering* is offered with the Peace-offering, of which the offerer, as well as the priests, partake ; [ii.] *leavened cakes also* are seen to be offered with the sacrifice, which, though presented "with the Peace-offering," are, of course, not burnt ; and [iii.] further *one cake out of the whole oblation,*—that is, one of each sort, both leavened and unleavened,—is, after being waved as a Heave-offering to the Lord, given to the priest, who sprinkles the blood of the Peace-offerings ; [iv.] the last thing noted

* Chapter vii. 12–17.

is, that the flesh of the offering is *to be eaten the same day,* or until the morning.   Three of these four particulars are entirely overlooked when the sacrifice of Peace-offerings is "*for a vow;*" and though the fourth is noticed, it is seen rather differently; the flesh in "the vow-offering" is *eaten for two days,* or until the third day.   As several of the emblems used here have already been considered, though not in the combination which we find in the Peace-offering, a few words may be sufficient to point out their purport and significance here.

[i.] In the offering "for praise," *a Meat-offering is offered of which the offerer as well as the priests partake.*   The purport of the Meat-offering, as we have already seen, is the fiulfilment of the second table of the Decalogue; man offering to God as a sweet savour the perfect accomplishment of his duty towards his neighbour.   The peculiarity here is, that the offerer partakes of this Meat-offering, a thing not permitted in the common Meat-offering.   The common Meat-offering shews us the fulfilment of the law, simply with reference to God, to satisfy Him.   But that same fulfilment of the law has other aspects, one of which is, that it satisfies the Offerer also.   This is the truth brought out in the Peace-offering, in which the Offerer, as well as God, finds satisfaction in the fulfilment of all righteousness.   And this satisfaction is not only in the fulfilment of that part of the law which had reference to God, and which was represented by the offering of a life; but in that part also which referred to man, and was represented by the unleavened cakes of the Meat-offering. The latter part of this appears to be quite lost sight of, unless the Peace-offering is apprehended as offered "for praise."

[ii.] But further, in the offering "for praise" *leavened cakes also are seen to be offered with the sacrifice.** This emblem, too, has already occupied our attention in "the leavened cakes" of the day of Pentecost. Those cakes represent the offering of the Church. When Christ's work is seen merely as "the vow," as a matter of service, the Church's offering does not come into sight: but when His offering is seen "for praise," that is for God's glory, the Church is seen united with Him. The leavened cakes could not be burnt to God, but they come before Him "*with*"† the sweet-savour offerings. And though not fit to stand the trial of fire, or to satisfy God as the meat of His altar, they are yet presented for His gracious acceptance, and are fed upon by the Priest and Offerer.

[iii.] And this leads us to the next particular, namely, that *one cake out of all the oblation* (that is, one of each sort, both leavened and unleavened,) *is given to the priest who sprinkles the blood,*‡ while the remainder, both of the leavened and unleavened, belongs to him who brings the offering. Christ, as Priest, finds food and satisfaction not only in His own blessed and perfect offering: He feeds also on "the leavened cake:" the offering of His Church, with all its failings, satisfies Him. As Offerer, too, He presents this offering with

* Verse 13.   † Chapter vii. 13, and xxiii. 18.   ‡ Verse 14.

His own : as Offerer, too, He feeds upon it. And we also, as offerers in Him, though not able to hold fellowship with God on the Church's offerings, (no part of leavened cake was burnt to God,) may yet find satisfaction in such offerings, even as Paul found satisfaction in the love of saints.* Sweet, however, as such offerings may be to us, and much as they may "refresh our bowels in the Lord," they cannot by themselves be accepted of God, or be the ground of our communion with Him. The only meat we can thus share with Him is the unblemished and perfect meat of the altar. But these particulars and distinctions are not apprehended, unless the Peace-offering is seen as offered "for praise."

[iv.] The last particular noticed respects *the period during which the Peace-offering was to be eaten.* The time for eating the offering "for praise" was "*the same day*" or "*until the morning*:"† in the "vow-offering" there is a little difference ; it might be eaten "*the same day and on the morrow,*" or "*until the third day.*"‡

Now the "morning" and the "third day" are sufficiently common types, and are both constantly used, I believe, to denote the resurrection.§ Thus far I con-

* 2 Timothy i. 16 ; Philemon 7, 20.
† Verse 15.   ‡ Verses 16, 17.
§ For "*the morning*" see Exod. xii. 8, 10 ; Psalm xlix. 14 ; Rom. xiii. 12. For "*the third day,*" Hosea vi. 2 ; Luke xiii. 32 ; 1 Cor. xv. 4, &c. The "*eighth day*" also is the resurrection, but the resurrection looked at in a different aspect, either to the view given in "*the morning*" or "*the third day.*"

ceive the sense of the emblems unquestionable : but I am not so certain as to the different aspect of the resurrection represented by each of them. I am disposed, however, to think that "*the morning*" represents the resurrection as the time of *Christ's appearing;* while the thought connected with "*the third day*" is simply *deliverance from the grave.* In either case the main truth remains the same, that the Peace-offering is our food until the resurrection : but in the one case we eat as those whose time is short, in the night it may be, but in hope of the morning ; in the other the thought of the morning is lost, and instead of it we see days of labour to intervene. I need not say that the first is the higher and happier view.

Such is the law of the Peace-offering, and such some of its chief varieties. In our progress we have little more than traced the outline, but how much does it contain. Even what we see and know of it reveals both depths and lengths of grace in the Redeemer ; when we think of what our peace cost Him, and that He poured out His life to bring us to communion. Blessed be His name for the measure and manner of His love. May He reveal it to us by the Holy Ghost. Well might the Psalmist say, " Praise waiteth for thee, O God, in Zion : and unto thee shall the vow be performed. Blessed is the man whom thou choosest, and causest to approach unto thee, that he may dwell in thy courts : we shall be satisfied with the goodness of thy house, even of thy holy temple."* " They shall

* Psalm lxv. 1, 4.

be abundantly satisfied with the fatness of thy house. Thou shalt make them drink of the river of thy pleasures."* The Lord grant us, not merely to know about these things, but to know Him better of whom they speak.

* Psalm xxxvi. 8.

THE SIN-OFFERING.

LEVITICUS IV., AND V. 1–13.

WE now come to OFFERINGS NOT OF A SWEET SAVOUR.
Of this class are the *Sin and Trespass-offerings ;* the
object of which is to present Christ's Offering to us
in an aspect wholly distinct from those already dwelt
upon.   Hitherto we have met no thought of Sin in
the offerings.   The Burnt-offering, the Meat-offering,
and the Peace-offering, much as they differed, were
yet alike in this, that in each of them the offering
was the presentation of something which was sweet
to Jehovah, an oblation to satisfy His holy requirements, and in the acceptance of which He found grate-
ful satisfaction.   But here, in the Sin and Trespass-
offerings, we read of Sin in connexion with the offering.
Here is confessed sin, judged sin, sin requiring sacrifice and blood-shedding ; yet sin atoned for, blotted
out, and pardoned.

It might perhaps be thought that this view of the
Offering, as leading to the knowledge and discovery of
sin, might be less blessed, less full of joy and consolation, than those views of the Offering on which we
have already meditated.   Such might be the case,

I

were we other than what we are, and were the Sin-
offering other than God has provided.   Were we sinless beings who knew no sin, this view of the Offering
might not be needed by us, save as revealing the grace
of Him who, though the Holy One, could be "just and
yet a justifier."   But to us, who, knowing ourselves
to be sinners, and as such subject to God's just wrath
and judgment, have yet believed in Him "who was
made a curse for us," * this view of the Offering is
perhaps of all most comforting.   The Sin-offering
shews that sin has been judged, and that therefore
the sense of sin, if we believe, need not shake our
sense of safety.   Sin is indeed here pre-eminently
shewn to be exceeding sinful, exceeding hateful, exceeding evil before God : yet it is also shewn to have
been perfectly met by sacrifice, perfectly borne, perfectly judged, perfectly atoned for.

And the fact is, that the view of Christ as Sin-
offering is sooner apprehended than those prefigured
in the Burnt and Meat-offerings.   Experience abundantly testifies this.   As in the type the Sin-offerings,
though last in order of institution, were invariably the
first in order of application ; † so in the experience of
saints, Christ is first apprehended as the Sin-offering.
Long before there is any intelligence of all the details
of Christ's perfect work, as fulfilling all righteousness

* Gal. iii. 13.

† See any chapter which describes the order in which the sacrifices were to be offered, as Exodus xxix.; Leviticus viii. ix. xiv. and
2 Chron. xxix, &c.

as man, and being accepted of God as a sweet-smelling savour,—long before there is any thought of His offering as that wherein God takes delight and finds satisfaction, the weak Christian sees Christ as Sin-bearer, and His offering as a sacrifice *for sin.* And though, as the type will shew us, this view may be very indistinct, confused, or partial,—and though it may be apprehended by different believers with an immense difference as to the measure of discernment and intelligence,—yet in some form or other it is, I may say invariably, the first view of Christ's Offering apprehended by the Christian.

I have observed that in the institution of the offerings, as recorded in the commencement of Leviticus, the sweet-savour offerings precede the others, but that in the application of these offerings, the order is reversed. I will add here a word or two on this point, as, if I mistake not, this, like all else, has a meaning in it. The reason of it will, I think, commend itself, when the characteristic difference of these offerings is seen. The sweet-savour offerings are, as we know, Christ in perfectness offering Himself for us to God *without sin :* the others, on the contrary, as we shall see, represent Him as offering Himself as our representative *for sin.* The *institution* of these sacrifices gives us certain aspects of the Offering, in the order in which they are viewed by God : and in this view Christ offering Himself without sin would clearly precede His offering Himself for sin. Had He not been in Himself what the Burnt and Meat-offerings typify,

a voluntary offerer of a sinless offering, He could **not**
have been offered for sin : the fact of His being perfect
fitted Him to be a Sin-offering.   But the *application*
of the offerings, on the other hand, gives us the order
of Christ's work as viewed by Israel; and Israel's
view in this case, as in all others, begins where the
Offering meets Israel's sin and failure.   For this
reason it is, I cannot doubt, that in their application
the Sin-offerings preceded the Burnt-offerings.

But to pass from this order to the Offerings themselves, the least degree of attention is sufficient to
shew, that *the offerings which were not of a sweet
savour are of two sorts,*—first *the Sin-offerings,** and
then *the Trespass-offerings.*†   For a Christian rightly
to know the difference between these, shews that he
has learnt more than one lesson in God's school.   And
indeed it is one mark,—a mark not to be mistaken,—
of the present low state of the mass of Christians, that
so many of them never seem to apprehend the difference which God sees between Sin and Trespass.   I
assume here that there is a difference; for with these
offerings before us, it is impossible to doubt it.   One
thing at least is plain : God sees a difference : happy
the saint who sees with God.   Happy, I say, for
though the knowledge of sin in itself can never be a
cause of joyfulness, yet to see and judge anything
as God Himself judges it is a step to blessedness, as
surely as it is a mark of communion with Him.   Truly
it is for lack of knowledge on the particular now

* Chapters iv. and v. 1–13.   † Chapter v. 14–19, vi. 1–7.

before us, that so many are mourning who should be praising; for they do not see that atonement has been made and accepted for sin in them, as well as for their acts of trespass. I defer, however, entering into this subject, until we have more fully considered the peculiar character of the Sin-offering. When we have done this, and obtained, as I hope, a clearer apprehension of it, we shall be better able to discriminate the distinction between Sin and Trespass and their respective offerings.

I proceed, therefore, at once to the consideration of THE SIN-OFFERING. We may look at it, first, *in its contrast to the other offerings;* and then, *in its several varieties:* the first will shew the particular aspect of Christ's Offering which is prefigured in the type now before us; the second, the various measures of intelligence with which this aspect may be apprehended by Christians.

I. To note then, first, the Sin-offering IN CONTRAST WITH THE OTHER OFFERINGS: three particulars will give us all the outlines. (1.) First, *it was, though without blemish, not of a sweet savour.* Then (2.) *it was burnt, not on the altar in the tabernacle, but on the bare earth without the camp:* in these two particulars the Sin-offering was in contrast to the Burnt-offering. Lastly, (3.) it was *an offering for sin, and this as distinct from an offering for trespass:* in this, as I need hardly observe, it stands contrasted particularly with the Trespass-offering.

(1.) First, *the Sin offering, though without spot or*

*blemish, was yet not a sweet savour offering.** I have already dwelt more than once on what is implied in a "sweet savour." I need not, therefore, here do more than refer to it, to shew how Jesus, the spotless One, could be "not a sweet savour."

The distinction is this:—the sweet-savour offerings were *for acceptance;* the others *for expiation.* In the first class, sin is not seen at all; it is simply the faithful Israelite satisfying Jehovah. In the Sin-offerings it is just the reverse; it is an offering charged with the sin of the offerer. In the Burnt-offering and other sweet-savour offerings, the offerer came as a worshipper, to give in his offering, which represented himself, something sweet and pleasant to Jehovah. In the Sin and Trespass-offerings, which were not of a sweet savour the offerer came as a convicted sinner, to receive in his offering, which represented himself, the judgment due to his sin or trespass. In the Sin-offerings, as in the Burnt-offerings, Christ is Offerer: but here He is seen standing for us under the imputation of sin. For though in Himself without sin, "the Holy One," yet He became our substitute, confessed our sins as His sins, and bore their penalty. Thus taking up His people's sins as His own, He says, "*My* sins, O God, are not hid from Thee."† "Innumerable evils have compassed me about; *mine* iniquities have taken hold upon me: they are more than the hairs of my head; therefore my heart faileth me."‡ O wondrous mystery, the Holy One of God made sin for sinners!§ And O unspeak-

* Chapter iv.   † Psalm lxix. 5.   ‡ Psalm xl. 12.   § 2 Cor. v. 21.

able love, the Blessed One made a curse for cursed ones !*

Such, then, is the import of the distinction between what was, and what was not, of a sweet savour. In the one case the offering was accepted to shew that the offerer was accepted of the Lord; and the total consumption of the offering on the altar shewed God's acceptance of, and satisfaction in, the offerer. In the other case the offering was cast out, and burnt, not on God's table, the altar, but in the wilderness without the camp; to shew that the offerer in his offering endures the judgment of God, and is cast out of His presence as accursed. In the one the offerer came to satisfy God, and having in his offering stood the sifting trial of fire, was accepted as a sweet savour, and fed upon, if I may say so, by the Lord. In the other he came as a guilty sinner, and in his offering bore the penalty for sin. The one is,—"He gave Himself for us, as an offering to God of a sweet-smelling savour."† The other,—"He gave Himself for our sins:"‡ "He was made sin for us, who knew no sin."§ The Sin-offering is the latter of these: not for acceptance, but to expiate sin.

And yet the Sin-offering needed to be "*without blemish,*"‖ as much as the Burnt-offering: indeed in no offering was perfectness more requisite. Again and again it is repeated that nothing but an unblemished victim could be a Sin-offering:¶ one blemish, either

* Gal. iii. 13.   † Eph. v. 2.   ‡ Gal. i. 4.   § 2 Cor. v. 21.
‖ Chapter iv. 3.   ¶ Chapter iv. 3, 23, 28, 32, &c.

within or without, was enough to unfit the offering **to** bear the sin of others.   So, because He was sinless, Jesus could be a Sin-offering.   Because He was perfect, He could bear our sin.

It is well to meditate on this, *the perfectness yet the rejection of the victim in the Sin-offering*, that we may learn how alone sin can be borne, and how it has been borne and pardoned.   Had there been spot or blemish of any sort on Jesus, His offering could not have met and expiated sin.   Had there been one desire in His heart unholy, one act, one word, one look, one thought imperfect, He could not have borne the curse for others : He would Himself have needed atonement.   But He was tried by man, by God, by devils ; and the trial only proved Him " the Holy One of God."   And " yet it pleased the Lord to bruise Him : "* though "the Holy One," He was cast without the camp : the only spotless offering this world ever witnessed, was yet not only afflicted of man, but judged of God and smitten.

The spotless Jesus not a sweet savour ! the spotless Jesus accursed of God ! cast forth, not merely without the Tabernacle, but as unclean " without the camp ! " " But He was wounded for our transgressions, He was bruised for our iniquities : the chastisement of our peace was upon Him ; and by His stripes we were healed." † Here we may learn the measure of the love of Jesus, and our security as having been already judged in Him. In His love He beheld, and saw us ruined, and that fallen man could not bear the curse and live : " Then He

* Isaiah liii. 10.   † Isaiah liii. 5.

said, Lo, I come:" and He came, and was accursed for sinners. As our representative He confessed our sins, binding on Him that which would have sunk us in wrath for ever: as our representative He bore their curse; and received at God's hand our judgment. And because He has been judged for us, justice is satisfied; we who believe have already been judged in Him; and God now is "*just to forgive us*,"* for Christ has borne our sins. "He His own self bare our sins in His own body on the tree, that we, being dead to sins, might live unto righteousness:"† "For in that He died, He died unto sin once; but in that He liveth, He liveth unto God. Likewise reckon ye yourselves to be dead indeed unto sin, but alive unto God in Jesus Christ our Lord."‡

But I pass on to the next characteristic feature in the Sin-offering, which has already been incidentally alluded to.

(2.) *The Sin-offering was burnt without the Camp.*§ The other offerings were, without exception, burnt on the altar in the Tabernacle. Here "the skin of the bullock, and all his flesh, with his head, and with his legs, his inwards, &c., even the whole bullock shall he carry without the camp, ... and burn him on the wood with fire."‖ The import of this we have more than once noticed in passing. It testified how completely the offering was identified with the sin it suffered for; so completely identified that it was itself looked

* 1 John i. 9.   † 1 Pet. ii. 24.   ‡ Rom. vi. 10, 11.
§ Chap. iv. 12, 21.   ‖ Verses 11, 12.

at as sin, and as such cast out of the camp into the wilderness. A part indeed, "the fat,"* was burnt on the altar, to shew that the offering, though made a sin-bearer, was in itself perfect. But the body of the victim, "*even the whole bullock*," was cast forth with-out the camp. "Wherefore Jesus also, that He might sanctify the people with His own blood, suffered with-out the gate."† He was cast out as one who was unfit for Jerusalem, as unworthy a place in the city of God.

And what this must have cost that Blessed One can never be entered into or understood, till the holiness of Christ and the sinfulness of sin are seen in measure at least as God sees them. Who shall tell the secrets of that hour, when this part of the type was fulfilled in Jesus; when He was led forth without the camp, to bear the vengeance due to sinners? His own words may perhaps help us to lift the veil :—"My God! my God! why hast Thou forsaken me?"‡ As a man,—and He was perfect man, with all our feelings and affec-tions, sin excepted,—as a man He felt the approach of death by painful, shameful, lingering suffering: but the hiding of His Father's face, the consequence of imputed sin; this was His anguish. Doubtless He suffered being tempted; He suffered from reproach, from the shame, the contempt, the spitting : doubtless He felt the mockery of His foes, the flight of His dis-ciples, with all their aggravating circumstances. How He felt let the Psalms reveal. But it was not this which made Him cry in anguish, "My God! my God!

* Verse 8.   † Heb. xiii. 12.   ‡ Matt. xxvii. 46.

why hast Thou forsaken me?" He had "suffered being tempted;"* He had "suffered, leaving us an example;"† but His greatest suffering was, "He suffered for sins."‡

And herein was His anguish, that He who had never known what it was to have a thought out of communion with His Father, should for a season be cast out of His presence, and endure the hiding of that Father's face. In the Garden, looking forward to this hour, with a will still longing for unbroken fellowship with His God, He cried once and again, while great drops of blood fell from Him,—"If it be possible, let this cup pass from me." But even here He says, "Nevertheless not my will,—not my will, but Thine, be done." § Yea, knowing what being forsaken of God would involve, He comes to His Father and says, "Not my will, but Thy will." He might, had He wished to spare Himself, have escaped this. He might have refused to drain the cup of trembling. But then how would His Father have been glorified,—how should we have been redeemed to His praise? Therefore "He suffered for sins," and "the Just One" died for the unjust. He took our place that we may take His: He was "cast out" that we might be "brought nigh" ‖ for ever. Blessed, blessed Lord, may we in the knowledge of Thy love learn to love Thee better!

What consolation is there here for the mourner groaning under the sense of sin or strong temptation; to know Jesus, though sinless, has suffered for sins,

* Heb. ii. 18. † 1 Pet. ii. 21. ‡ 1 Pet. iii. 18.
§ Luke xxii. 42. ‖ Eph. ii. 13.

and therefore He can, and assuredly will, sympathize
with us.   And oh! what security, too, is here: our
sins have a Sin-bearer; they were once His burden.
It is unbelief, or ignorance of the Sin-bearer, that
leaves the sense of the burden but for a moment upon
us.   Faith sees the Sin-offering "without the camp,"
and that Jesus there has met, and suffered for sins
for us.

(3.) The third peculiarity we may note in the Sin-
offering is, that *it was an offering for sin, not an
offering for trespass.**   This distinction, like all the
rest which God has recorded, is full of instruction and
of comfort to our souls.   It is as definite, too, as any
of the other differences which we have dwelt upon.
The want of apprehension respecting it only arises
from our so little knowing either what man is, or what
God is.   With our shortsightedness, our inability to
see beyond the surface, we naturally look at *what man
does* rather than at *what he is;* and while we are
willing to allow that *he does* evil, we perhaps scarcely
think that *he is* evil.   But God judges *what we are* as
well as *what we do; our sin,* the sin in us, as much
as *our trespasses.*   In His sight sin in us, *our evil
nature,* is as clearly seen as our trespasses, which are
but *the fruit* of that nature.   He needs not wait to see
the fruit put forth.   He knows the root is evil, and so
will be the buddings.

Now the distinction between the Sin and Trespass-

* Chapter iv. 3, 21, 24, 33, compared with chapter v. 13, 19, and
vi. 2, 6.

offerings is just this :—the one is for sin in our nature,
the other for the fruits of it. And a careful examina-
tion of the particulars of the offerings is all that is
needed to make this manifest. Thus in the Sin-offering
no particular act of sin is mentioned, but *a certain
person* is seen standing confessedly as a sinner : in the
Trespass-offering *certain acts* are enumerated, and *the
person* never appears. In the Sin-offering I see a person who needs atonement, offering an oblation *for himself* as a sinner : in the Trespass-offering I see certain
acts which need atonement, and the offering offered *for
these particular offences*. The details of the offerings,
as we examine them, will bring all this before us most
remarkably. Of course, in the Sin-offering, though the
man is seen rather than his acts, proof must needs be
brought that he is a sinner. But let it be noticed that
this is done, not by the enumeration of certain trespasses, but simply by a reference to the law ; which,
though no particular transgression is mentioned, is said
to have been neglected or broken.* Be it noticed, no
particular act is mentioned, though of course it is by
particular acts that sin in us is shewn ; but the particular acts are not seen in the Sin-offering, for the object is to shew sin, not trespass. And therefore, though
it was needful to shew sin, and in doing so to refer to
the commandment as exposing it, yet any definite act
of trespass is not seen here : for it is " an offering *for
sin*," not an offering *for trespass*. In the Trespass-
offering, on the other hand, it is exactly the reverse.

* Chapter iv. 2, 13, 14, 22, 27, &c.

We have nothing but one detail after another of particular wrongs and offences; the first class being of wrongs done against God, the other of wrongs against our neighbour.

And here, by the way, let me call attention to a point incidentally brought before us respecting the Sin-offering, namely, that the sin was brought out " by the commandment," as it is said, " If he shall sin through ignorance against any of the commandments." * We get here, I think, the reason why before the law there were neither Sin nor Trespass-offerings. We read indeed of Burnt-offerings and Meat-offerings being offered by many of the early patriarchs; but they are never recorded to have offered Sin-offerings, for "where there is no law there is no transgression."† " By the law," says the Apostle, " is the knowledge of sin," and again, " *Sin is not imputed* where there is no law." ‡ It was the law which convicted man of sin, and made it necessary that he should have a Sin-offering. " The law entered that the offence might abound; but where sin abounded grace

* Verse 2, &c.

† Rom. iv. 15. I observe that in Job (chap. i. 5.) we find the Burnt-offering offered in reference to sin. We read that " Job rose up early in the morning, and offered Burnt-offerings according to the number of them all : for Job said, It may be that my sons have sinned, and cursed God in their hearts." This was before the law was given; so Job says, " *It may be* that my sons have sinned." Had they sinned after the giving of the law, a Sin or Trespass-offering would have been needed; but before the law the Burnt-offering was all which could be given: and as it represented all God's claim fulfilled, nothing more in such an age could be added to it.

‡ Rom. iii. 20, and v. 13.

did much more abound."* The law entered, and it
proved man a sinner, and that to make his flesh other
than sinful flesh was impossible. But grace has done
what law could not do; grace brought One "in the
likeness of sinful flesh, and for sin,"† to save us. The
truth is, the law given by Moses was given neither to
make nor prove man holy; but rather to prove us, what
God ever since the fall has seen us, in ourselves sinners
and only sinners. Yet how has Satan beguiled man
here also : he would have us to prove ourselves holy by
that which God gave to prove us sinners.

But to return to the distinction between the Sin and
Trespass-offering :—the one was for sin in our nature,
the other for the fruits of it. In the Sin-offering, the
atonement is seen not for trespasses the fruits of sin,
but for sin itself within us. I would that all God's
children saw this. Sure I am,—and the type proves it,
—that many know the Trespass-offering who have but
very imperfect views of Christ as Sin-offering. I do
not now speak of the unconverted : with them acts of
trespass are the only things discernible : sin in them is
generally utterly disbelieved ; at all events its guilt is
always unfelt, unrecognized. With the young Christian,
too, but just awakened, how much less perception is
there of sin than trespass : *he has done* this evil, or
that evil, or the other ; he scarcely has learnt as yet that
in himself *he is* evil. But look at the man who has
somewhat grown in grace ; not only what he has done,
but what he is, is his sorrow. With such it is not so

* Rom. v. 20. † Rom. viii. 3.

much this or that act of trespass, which leaves the question of guilt on the conscience : but it is the constant sense of indwelling evil, and that "when we would do good, evil is present with us." This or that particular act of iniquity we have confessed, it is past, and we believe it pardoned : but this ever-remaining, ever-struggling sin within us, it is this more than ought else that burdens us. True, "the Spirit in our hearts cries Abba, Father," and "the Spirit in us lusteth against the flesh ;" but we find that all this instead of improving the flesh only manifests it, and shews how it "lusteth against the Spirit." * To those who are thus painfully learning *what they are,* what joy to know Christ died for this as well as for trespasses ; and that this indwelling sin, as much as our acts of wickedness, was equally confessed and put away by His sacrifice. Nay, had we not been suffering under this very evil, had we been without this sin, He would not have offered a Sin-offering. It was because we were this that He offered ; and because He offered, we who trust Him are saved.

Oh, how little is this apprehended, and, consequently, how little peace is there among saints! Many seem to think that the Spirit's work in revealing to them their sinfulness,† should be an excuse for unbelief and doubtings ; that because God in His mercy has shewn them what they are, sinners, therefore they are not safe. To such I say,—Are we saved by Christ as sinners, or are we saved by being sinless and holy ? God's testimony

* Gal. v. 17.   † " He shall convince of sin," &c., John xvi. 8.

is that we are saved as sinners, not by the Spirit's work in us, but by Christ's work for us. The Lord grant us to know more of the Spirit's work in us ; but after all, this is not the ground of peace. The type is clear on this : and if it shews anything, it shews that the discovery of sin should not shake the believer's faith of pardon ; for faith sees not only that we have sinned, but that the "Holy One" has been made sin for us. To doubt our pardon because we see our sin is just weakness of faith in the Offering : it proves how low is our estimate of Christ, how limited our confidence in God's love and faithfulness.

Do I then speak lightly of sin ? God forbid ! If we want to know how hateful it is, we have but to look at the Sin-offering ; to see the Holy One of God, His beloved Son, for sin cast out and broken. Our sin is indeed hateful to God, but it does not alter the value of Christ's Offering. Our sin indeed is most hateful ; but I ask still, has not the Sin-offering been offered ? If it has not, then we may mourn for ever, for we can never blot out one single trespass. But if it has been offered, what are all our doubts but aspersions on the value of Christ's Offering ? Whatever plea we have for them,—be it humility, or fear of presumption, or the amount and evil of our sinfulness,—God judges such pleas for doubt as unbelief, and as a questioning of what He testifies of Jesus. God indeed never forgets we are sinners : we may forget it, He never can : but He never forgets the Offering of Christ, and that by that Offering the Church's sins are cancelled. And the

K

blood of the Sin-offering which is taken within the veil,
by the High Priest on the great day of atonement,
remains there where none can approach to hide it, ever
present before the eye of God.   And even when through
the uncleanness of the camp or the wilderness we seem
to lose sight of it, it remains there before Him a
witness that sin has been judged, and that the way is
open for sinners into the holiest.

"He by Himself purged our sins."* Yea, He sat
not down again in glory till He had purged them.
What certainty of salvation is there here for those who
trust in Jesus? It is no future work, no promised
work, no work to be yet accomplished, but a finished
work which is our sure foundation.   "He bore our
sins:" this is God's testimony: and having borne
them "He was raised *because we were justified.*"†
Had we not been justified, Christ could not have been
raised. His resurrection, and ours in Him, is the
proof that we are justified. If sin has not been already
borne, how shall it be borne? Is Christ to die again,
is He to be again a Sin-offering? "Christ was ONCE
offered to bear the sins of many,"‡ and "now there re-
maineth no more sacrifice for sin."§ If therefore He
has not borne our sins, He can never bear them. If He
has borne them, why have we not peace? If we think

* Heb. i. 3.

† Rom. iv. 25. "He was delivered, παρεδόθη διὰ τὰ παραπτώματα
ημῶν, *because of* our sins; and raised, ηγέρθη διὰ τὴν δικαίωσιν
ἡμῶν, *because of* our justification."

‡ Heb. ix. 28.   § Heb. x. 18, 26.

that the Sin-offering once offered on Calvary has not met all sin and every trespass, whatsoever remains, be it small or great, can never be propitiated, never pardoned. But Jesus for His people bore not some sins, but all sins: and "by Him all that believe are justified from *all* things."* "He hath forgiven us *all* trespasses."† The Cross has cancelled all. May the Lord more fully reveal these things to His chosen ones, that their rejoicing may be, not Yea and Nay, but Yea and Amen.

Such is the general character of the Sin-offering, as elicited by comparing the particulars in which it stands in contrast to the other Offerings. We now proceed to consider,

II. THE VARIETIES IN THIS OFFERING, which shew the different apprehensions which may be entertained of this particular aspect of Christ's sacrifice.

And here there is very great variety, far exceeding what we find in any of the preceding offerings. In the Sin-offering there is not only variety seen in *the animal offered*, and in the details which are given as to the mode of offering it; but a good deal of variety is noticed as to *the person of the offerer*, a peculiarity not to be found in any of the other offerings. Besides these varieties, there are several other minor ones, in reference to the *blood*, the *fat*, the *body*, and lastly the *name*, of the offering. Each of these varieties as they are recorded by the Lord, so will they be found worthy of our attentive meditation. I shall do little more here

* Acts xiii. 39. † Col. ii. 13.

than mark some of the chief outlines, and may the
Lord make His people to profit by them.

(1.) The first variety, then, which is seen in the Sin-
offering is *the difference in the animal offered*. In the
Burnt-offering we observed a similar variety ; the purport of which is, of course, the same in both cases.
There is, however, far greater variety in the different
grades of the Sin-offering than in the Burnt-offering ;
thus teaching us that Christ's offering for sin may be
apprehended with far greater measures of difference
than Christ as Burnt-offering. In the Burnt-offering,
the offering though varied was limited, either to a
bullock, a *lamb*, a *goat*, or *turtle-doves*.* Here in the
Sin-offering we have several other grades,† coming
down at last to a sin-offering composed of simple
"*flour.*" The last grade is this :—"And if he be not
able to bring two turtle-doves or two young pigeons ;
then he that sinned shall bring for his offering the
tenth part of an ephah of fine flour for a sin-offering :
he shall put no oil upon it, neither shall he put any
frankincense thereon ; for it is a sin-offering."

We have already considered the import of these
varied emblems ; I need not therefore do more than
just advert to them. Suffice it to say that here, as in
the Burnt-offerings, they shew us the different characters under which the Offering of Christ may be
apprehended by us. In the Sin-offering as in the

* See chapter i.
† "A male kid," chapter iv. 23 : "a female kid," iv. 28 : "a
female lamb," iv. 32 : ending at last with "flour," v. 11.

Burnt-offering, one saint has one view, another another view respecting the character of the offering. One sees the willing labour, another the submission, another the innocence, of the Offering which is yielded to Jehovah. But in the Sin-offering we have still lower views, the lowest of which is, as we have observed, very like a Meat-offering. The solution is easy. As in the preceding offerings we found, without exception, that there was an indistinctness, almost like confusion, in the lower views,—a mixing up of one aspect wi*h another, while the distinct thought of each was more or less lost sight of; so is it here: in its lowest grade, (the one we are considering,) the Sin-offering is seen very nearly as a Meat-offering. The thought is almost that of the Meat-offering, yet it is seen as offered for sin: this is distinctly noticed: though "of flour," "*it is a Sin-offering.*" *

How exactly this peculiarity in the type describes the way in which some apprehend the Offering, will be best understood by those who, going from strength to strength, have learnt how partially Christ may be apprehended, even by those who love Him. Some see the pain and sorrow Christ had in service, the grinding, the bruising, the scorching, of the Meat-offering: and they think that this was His sin-bearing: they cannot distinguish between the trials of service and the curse. They see indeed a life of suffering, but they do not see One accursed for them. Nevertheless, they see a suffering One offered, and though they lose many points in

* Chapter v. 11.

His Offering, they still see it as offered for sin. **Yet** how much is lost, in such partial views, of the design and character of the work of Jesus.

(2.) The next variety we may notice is in *the person offering:* we have the priest, the congregation, the ruler, and the common Israelite. First in order we have the Sin-offering for *the priest;** then the Sin-offering for *the whole congregation;*† then the Sin-offering for *a ruler;*‡ then for *one of the common people;* § and lastly, the Sin-offering for *particular sins;* ‖ in which last *the person of the offerer* is lost sight of, and the *particular act* for which he offers more clearly seen. This last is very nearly akin to the Trespass-offering, and is indeed called indifferently by both names of Sin and Trespass. ¶ In this last class, as in the lowest classes of the other offerings, we get the lowest view which can be taken of this particular aspect of the Offering.

But what is the import of this variety in *the person offering?* We have only to remember what these varieties are. They are, as we have sufficiently seen, only different measures of apprehension. In the Burnt-offering, the Meat-offering, and the Peace-offering, we have already become familiar with the varieties in *the Offering*, and have seen that they represent the different apprehensions which may be, and are, formed of its value and character. So in the Sin-offering, **the**

* Chapter iv. 3–12.   † Chapter iv. 13–21.
‡ Chapter iv. 22–26.   § Chapter iv. 27–35.
‖ Chapter v. 1–13.   ¶ Chapter v. 6–9.

varieties which are noted of *the Offerer*, in like manner represent the different apprehensions which are formed of the person who offered. Of course the Offerer here, as elsewhere, is Christ, man under the law, our representative. As such He is here seen confessing sin; but though seen as Offerer in this aspect, He may yet be seen very differently. For example, in the first case the offerer is apprehended as "priest," a person who stands the representative of *a family* or *congregation*. In other cases the offerer is seen as "one of the common people," one who stands simply the representative of *an individual*. In the lowest cases of all, the person of the offerer is altogether lost sight of, neither individual nor congregation are seen, and *the sin* for which he suffers is almost the only thing apprehended.

But let us note here a little more particularly, the exact difference which is intended by these separate views of the Offerer; and that we may see the contrast more clearly, let us for a moment set side by side the higher and lower grades of the Sin-offering.

In the first class the offerer is the "anointed priest;" in the next, "the whole congregation;" in a lower grade, (how great the contrast,) the offerer is "one of the common people." The "anointed priest," and "the whole congregation," are types familiar to the youngest Christian. "The anointed priest," as head of the priestly family, and the appointed mediator between God and man, stands the type of Jesus as head of a priestly family, and also as mediator to God's chosen Church. In this class, Christ, as Offerer of the Sin-offering, is seen either as Head of the Church, or as its appointed Mediator. His Offering is apprehended, not merely as the atonement for this or that individual, but as affecting a whole family or people. In the next class, "the congregation" offer. This congregation represents the Church. Here we lose sight of the priest as under the guilt of sin with Israel; but with this exception, the congregation's offering is almost identical with the preceding one. But the point to be especially noted in both these cases, and where they differ so remarkably from the others, is that the sin, and atonement made, is seen, not as affecting an individual merely, but the whole of Israel. Now, mark the contrast. In the lower classes the offerer is a private individual, "one of the common people:" and his sin, and the atonement made for it, is seen as affecting only himself. Those saints who have the highest views of the Sin-offering, see it as affecting not themselves merely, but the Priest and Israel. Those with lower views only see it for themselves: the High Priest's or Israel's interest in it is unseen and forgotten.

Here then is the difference. The apprehension some have of Christ as Offerer of the Sin-offering is One who in His own person represented the whole Church; the Church being seen either as the family of the Priest, or as the whole congregation of Israel. Others again see Him as head of a tribe, "the ruler;" in this case the unity of the Church is lost sight of. Others, far more numerous, never see anything of this:

Christ as Offerer of the Sin-offering is viewed as having stood for them individually. Others again, lower still in the scale of intelligence, see only that He stood for sin. These stages in the apprehension and experience of Christians, will be familiar to those who know much of that experience.

Such is the variety respecting the person of the Offerer, and such too, if I mistake not, the purport of it. We have only glanced at the outlines, but the details are equally full of interest; requiring indeed a certain measure of intelligence to apprehend them, yet if apprehended, precious to our souls. And just as every difference of *the Offering*,—the difference, I mean, whether it was a bullock, a lamb, or turtle-dove,—all brought before us some feature of Christ's work or character, in which both God and His saints saw perfectness; so here, in each of these varieties in *the Offerer*, there is some fresh thought or view of Christ's person for us to glory in. I will not, however, enter further into the consideration of them, not from a doubt of their value, but from a sense of the length to which they would carry me. I only pray that we may be led to feel our need of knowing more of Him of whom these things testify.

(3.) A third variety in the Sin-offering has reference to "*the blood*." *In the higher classes the blood was sprinkled on the incense altar;* * *in the lower classes it was not taken into the holy place, but sprinkled upon the brazen altar in the court.*† I fear it will be

* Chapter iv. 7, 18.   † Chapter iv. 25, 30, 34.

impossible to make this intelligible to those who have never considered the typical import of the relative parts of the Tabernacle. Two things, at least, must be apprehended; first, the import of these altars, and then of their sprinkling.

As to the altars, they were, the one of gold, the other brazen. The brazen one stood in the outer court of the congregation. The other, the golden one, in the holy place, where none but the priests might enter. The "outer court," with its brazen altar and laver, represents the earth and the work which is done in it to God-ward. The "holy place," with the golden altar for incense, shews us the heavenly places and their appointed service. On the brazen altar were offered the sacrifices of Israel. Any Israelite, if clean, might draw nigh and offer there.* But priests only might approach the golden altar, and nothing come on it save the perfumed incense.† The position and use of these altars, and the references to them in the New Testament,‡ unite to point out their typical meaning; the one leading us to the service of the Church as on earth, the other to their service as priests in heavenly places.

Thus much for the altars. As to the sprinkling of blood, I need scarcely say it always refers to atonement by sacrifice: it signifies that the thing or person sprinkled is thereby brought from a state of distance from God to a state of nearness. The sprinkling,

* Exodus xxix. 36–43.   † Exodus xxx. 1–10.
‡ Heb. xiii. 10, 16; Rev. viii. 3, 4, &c.

then, of blood upon the incense altar implied that until this act was performed the altar was unapproachable; and consequently, that all priestly service, and therefore all service of all kinds, was stopped between God and Israel. In like manner the sprinkling of blood on the brazen altar implied that till this was done, that altar too was regarded as unapproachable. In each case sin is apprehended to have interrupted communion; in the one, the communion of priests; in the other, that of Israel; while the sprinkling of blood declares that communion restored through the Sin-offering, on the incense altar to the priests, on the brazen altar to Israel.

The import of the distinction we are considering will now, I suppose, be sufficiently plain. In the higher classes, where it is observed that the incense altar needs sprinkling, the consequences of sin are seen to be far more extensive than in the other case; for the interruption of communion is apprehended, not of individuals on earth merely, but of the priests in their access to God as in heavenly places. In the lower classes, for instance, in the case of "one of the common people," it is not seen that sin has destroyed the communion of the congregation: it is not observed how the priest and Israel are implicated in it: the thought is rather about self. In a word, in the lower classes both the full effects, and the full remedy of sin, are known but partially. Need of personal acceptance and reconciliation is indeed seen, and that acceptance and reconciliation apprehended; but that the whole congre-

gation needs reconciliation, and that it has it, is unknown, or at least forgotten.   Thus is the sense of the
extent of the evil caused by sin exactly in proportion
to the depth of apprehension respecting the extent of
the reconciliation effected by the Sin-offering.   He
only that saw the Priest's altar hallowed for service by
the blood of the Sin-offering, saw also that the communion of that altar had ever been hindered by sin.
It is so on all points.   The deeper the apprehension of
the efficacy of the blood, the deeper will be the sense
of that from which it delivers us.

But the difference in the apprehension of this
particular goes even further.   In the fifth chapter,
which gives the lowest grades of the Sin-offering,
*there is no notice whatever taken of either altar.**
All that is apprehended is, that an atonement has
been made by the Priest; the altars, and their restoration to service, are forgotten.   This, alas! is the
common case with many now-a-days.   An atonement
has been made for sin; thus much they see, and they
are thankful for it.   But as for any intelligent apprehension of the different altars, or how far their use is
hindered by sin and restored by the Sin-offering, they
not only know nothing about it, but judge such
matters non-essential, unnecessary.   The same spirit

* Chapter v. 6.   "And he shall bring his trespass-offering unto
the Lord, for his sin which he hath sinned, a female from the flock,
a lamb, or a kid of the goats, for a sin-offering; and the priest shall
make an atonement for him concerning his sin."   It will be observed
that here there is no notice of *either altar.*

which makes the fool say, "There is no God," tempts even Christians to say there is nought in much He wrought for us.

(4.) A fourth variety noticed in the Sin-offering has reference to *"the fat." In the higher grades the fat was burnt upon the altar :* * *in the lowest class* † *this is overlooked : what was done with the fat is entirely unnoticed.* As usual between the highest and lowest class, we have several steps of more or less intelligence. In the first grade not only is it seen that the fat is burnt, but there is the fullest discrimination of every portion of it.‡ In the subsequent grades too, indeed in all save the lowest, the fat is burnt, but the parts are not discriminated. In the last grade alone of all, "the fat" of the offering is quite unnoticed. "The fat," as we have already seen in the other offerings, § represents the general health and energy of the whole body. Its being burnt to God was the appointed proof that the victim offered for sin was yet in itself acceptable. This acceptability is most seen in the higher classes, but it is apprehended also in all save the lowest grade. There the atonement made for sin is indeed apprehended, but the perfect acceptableness of the victim is unnoticed. So with some Christians, is not their thought respecting

---

* Chapter iv. 8, 9, 10, 19, 26, 31, 35.   † Chapter v. 6.

‡ Chapter iv. 8, 10. We read here of "the fat that covereth the inwards, and all the fat that is upon the inwards, and the fat that is upon the kidneys," &c. &c. In no other grade do we find this detail.

§ See in the Burnt-offering, p. 55.

the Sin-offering more of our pardon than of Christ's
perfectness?

(5.) Another variety we may observe in the Sin-
offering has reference to "*the body*" of the victim. *In
the higher grades it is cast without the camp:* * *in
the lower this is unnoticed: but in the law of the offer-
ings† another particular is marked: the priest is seen
to feed on the offering.* The import of this distinction
is at once obvious. Where the Sin-offering is fully
apprehended, the victim, which is the sin-bearer, is seen
accursed, and as such cast out as unclean into the
wilderness. Where the Sin-offering is more partially
apprehended, the victim is still seen as sin-bearer, but
the reality of its separation from God is lost sight of,
and its death viewed merely as satisfying the Mediator.

And here let me observe how amidst all this variety
of detail, there is still throughout one point of remarkable similarity in principle. It is this. In the lower
classes, that is where there is a lower measure of intelligence, the view of the *nature* of the Offering is
invariably exchanged for a view of the *effects* of it: in
other words, the Offering is seen as it affects Israel,
rather than as it is in itself, in its real character. Thus
the burning of the fat, shewing the perfectness of the
victim offered; and the casting forth of its body, shewing the nature of the judgment borne by it; these and
similar details respecting the sacrifice itself, are lost
sight of in the lower classes; while the effects of it, as
making atonement, are perhaps even more fully dwelt

* Chapter iv. 12, 21.   † Chapter vi. 25–30.

upon. And how exactly this accords with the successive
stages of Christian experience, will be sufficiently understood by those who know much either of themselves or
others. At first Christ's work, or person, or offering,
is viewed with interest solely on account of what it is to
us. Nothing respecting it is regarded as worthy of
notice save its bearing upon us, or efficacy towards us.
It has taken away our sins ; it has made atonement ;
this is the one thing, and almost the sole thing, seen
respecting it. Anything further than this at such a
stage would appear a grand impertinence. But let the
question of peace with God be settled, let our acceptance
become a thing known and realized, then the perfectness of the Offering, and what it is in itself, will, without exception, be more seen and dwelt upon.

(6.) The last variety I will here notice in the different
grades of the Sin-offering, is connected with *the name*
by which the offering is variously designated. *In the
higher classes it is always called a "Sin-offering,"**
and no particular act of trespass is noticed ; *in the
lower classes it is called a "Trespass-offering" as
well as a "Sin-offering,"*† and the person of the
offerer is lost sight of in the particular trespass. So
when the measure of apprehension is limited, there
will be want of intelligence respecting the precise
difference of sin and trespass ; nor this alone ; the
Offering will be seen only *for sins ;* that it is offered
for persons will not be apprehended.

But the expressions here used respectively, in reference

* Chapter iv. 8, 21, 24, 29.   † Chapter v. 6, 7.

to the effects of each different grade of the Sin-offering,
are so remarkably varied in reference to this particular,
that we cannot but notice the differences.   In the
higher class, in "the congregation's offering,"* we
simply read,—"The priest shall make atonement *for
them*."   In the case of "the ruler,"† we find this
slight variety,—"The priest shall make atonement *for
him for his sin*."   In the case of "one of the common
people,"‡ we find still further difference,—"The priest
shall make an atonement *for his sin which he hath
committed*."   Observe, in the first of these the atonement is seen *for persons ;*—"The priest shall make
atonement *for them*."   Of course the atonement here
is in consequence of sin, but *the persons* rather than
the sin are specially thought of.   In the next class, the
atonement is regarded as *for the sin of the persons*,
rather than for the persons ; though both persons and
sins are seen atoned for : as it says,—"The priest shall
make atonement *for him for his sin*."   In the lowest
class, "of the common people," the atonement for
persons is quite lost sight of ; "*the sin which he hath
committed* " is the chief thing dwelt upon.

How much is there "for our learning" in these
varieties ; how clearly they teach us the cause of the
difference in the views of saints respecting the Atonement.   There are some believers who see atonement for
sin, but almost deny that atonement has been made for
persons.   They see Christ gave Himself "*for sins*,"§
but hardly think He stood *for persons*.   In word

* Verse 20.   † Verse 26.   ‡ Verse 35.   § 1 Pet. iii. 18.

perhaps they assent to the Apostle, who said, " He loved *me*, and gave Himself *for me ;"** but the full reality and force of his words are scarcely assented to ; they need to be explained away. And as long as there are different measures of intelligence, so long will such difference of views be inevitable ; for though the truth is but one, yet while " we know in part," that one truth may and will be seen variously or partially.

Such are some of the Varieties in the Sin-offering. There are others to be seen, but I have noticed the chief. They shew us how very different is the measure of apprehension with which Christ as Sin-bearer may be seen by Christians. They shew us, too, how much of Christ, and therefore of joy, is lost sight of, by those who are content to continue in comparative ignorance of the Offering. I shall rejoice if these Notes should be used of God to lead but one of His people to seek more communion with Him, there to inquire whether these things are so, in deeper acquaintance with Him of whom they speak. Need I add here that it is one thing to know Him; another to know about Him. It is possible that some, who read these pages, may at once confess that such and such things are to be seen of Christ, who yet may have never seen, and even do not care to see, one of them. To know that another has seen the Prince, and know Him in His different relations, or that He may be so seen by those who dwell with Him, is very different from our knowing Him ourselves. It is just so with the knowledge of

* Gal. ii. 20.

L

Jesus.   Strangers to His family and household may hear about Him; but to know Him, as He is, must be taught of God, and is only to be learnt in His presence by His family.

We have thus gone through the particulars of the Sin-offering, as far at least as they are given in the Law of the Offerings.   In other places there are some other details added, the principles of which are, however, all contained in what we have investigated.   The additions only give us some new combinations as to the character under which the Sin-offering may be exhibited : I refer to the Offerings of *the Red Heifer,** and of *the Scape-goat* on the great day of Atonement.†   The offering of the Red Heifer, as we might expect from its being found in Numbers, exhibits not so much what the offering is in itself, as its use in meeting the wants of the wilderness.   Thus no memorial of it was burnt on the altar, nor was the blood seen to be taken into the Tabernacle; but the whole animal was burnt without the camp, and its ashes laid up to be mixed with the water of purification.   Then when an Israelite found himself unclean, through contact with the dead, these ashes with water were sprinkled on him.   All this is the Sin-offering as meeting our need of cleansing, and as given to remove the defilement caused by the dead things of the wilderness.   The view presented by it has to do with the effects of the offering, and its use towards man as applied by water, that is the Spirit.   In the Scape-goat, offered on the great day of atonement, the

* Numbers xix.   † Leviticus xvi.

view presented is very different. In this Sin-offering, which was offered but once a year, the blood was seen to be put on the mercy-seat. The offering it spoke of is shewn by Paul to have been "once for ever," and "access into the holiest" the consequence of it.* But I forbear going further into these particulars, as we have already sufficiently seen their principles. He that has apprehended what we have gone over will see more. For others, any further detail would be unintelligible.

Such is the Sin-offering, and such some of the apprehensions of it. Blessed be God that we have such an Offering. "He hath made Him to be sin for us who knew no sin; that we might be made the righteousness of God in Him."

* Heb. x. 1, 22.

THE TRESPASS-OFFERING.

LEVITICUS v. 14–19, and vi. 1–7.

WE now come to the TRESPASS-OFFERING. Closely allied in its broad principle to the Sin-offering, in certain particulars it as decidedly differs from it. These particulars, though few in number, are broadly marked, and full of teaching. . The apprehension of them will bring out very definitely that distinct aspect of Christ which the Trespass-offering is designed to present to us.

I proceed at once, as before, to consider this Offering, first, in its distinctive character, and then in its varieties: the first will give us the distinct aspect of Christ which is intended by this particular offering: the second shew the various apprehensions which may be formed of this one aspect.

I. First then, AS TO THE DISTINCTIVE CHARACTER OF THIS OFFERING: four particulars may at once be noted; the first having reference to the broad distinction between the Trespass-offerings and the whole class of sweet-savour offerings; the next bearing on the general distinction between the offerings not of a sweet savour, namely, the Sin and Trespass-offerings: the other two are more definite, and have to do with certain details connected with and flowing from the distinction between the nature of sin and trespass, and their atonement.

(1.) On the first particular I need not here enter, for the distinction between what was and what was not of a sweet savour has so often been dwelt upon. I therefore merely notice the fact that the Trespass-offering was *not a sweet savour*. Christ is seen here suffering for sins: the view of His work in the Trespass-offering is expiatory.

(2.) The next particular, too, we have already considered, namely, that *this offering was a Trespass-offering, as distinct from a Sin-offering*. We may, however, again advert to this, as the particulars given here very definitely mark what constitutes trespass. If a man wronged God, that was trespass: if he wronged or robbed his neighbour, that was trespass. We read,—"If a soul commit a trespass, and sin through ignorance, in the holy things of the Lord; .... then he shall make amends for the harm that he hath done." * Again,— "If a soul sin, and commit a trespass against the Lord, and lie unto his neighbour in that which was delivered him to keep, or in fellowship, or in a thing taken away by violence, or hath deceived his neighbour; or have found that which was lost, and lieth concerning it, and sweareth falsely; in any of all these that a man doeth, sinning therein: then it shall be, because he hath sinned, and is guilty, that he shall restore that which

* Chapter v. 15, 16.

he took violently away, or the thing which he hath
deceitfully gotten, or that which was delivered him to
keep, or the lost thing which he found." * Here trespass
is defined as *wrong done* to God, or *wrong done to* a
neighbour : we read of "*violently taking,*" "*deceitfully
getting,*" and "*swearing falsely about that which is
found.*" In every case of trespass, wrong was done ;
there was an *act of evil* by which another was injured.
And the offering for this act, the Trespass-offering, (in
this a contrast to the Sin-offering,) was offered by the
offerer, not because *he was,* but because *he had done,*
evil.   Accordingly, in the Trespass-offering we never
get sight of *any particular person* as a sinner : the *act
of wrong* is the point noticed and dwelt upon.

Such was trespass, actual wrong and robbery, and
yet there might be trespass, as well as sin, of which
the trespasser was ignorant.†   This is remarkable.
It shews how little man's judgment, not only respecting
what he is, but respecting what he does, can be trusted.
I observe that this unwitting trespass is specially seen
in cases of "wrong in holy things ;" we do not find
an instance of it in cases of "wrong done to a neighbour." The reason is manifest : our natural conscience
takes cognizance of man and his claims far more
readily than it is brought to understand God's standard for all approaches to Him in holy things. Thus
when little is known of this standard, when little is
seen of the holy things, when trespass is thought of
merely as affecting man, then unwitting trespass will

* Chapter vi. 2–4.   † Chapter v. 15, 17, 19.

not be recognized. But let a man be led much into the sanctuary, and learn something there of God's holiness, and he will find that the holy things themselves, the very opportunities of worship, may, through our weakness, open a door for trespass. Those who are most with God will most confess, what to some seems quite incredible, that often there has been unwitting trespass in the holiest acts of work and worship. I believe there is not an act of any kind, whether of praise, or prayer, or worship, or ministry, which may not, through Satan's cunning, prove an occasion to the flesh to bring forth some fruit of trespass. I need not particularize instances; I doubt not each instructed Christian will recognize some, where that which has been done either to the Lord or for the Lord, has afterwards been discovered to have been mixed with trespass. At the time, perhaps, the trespass has been unrecognized: but other circumstances or fuller light have made us conscious of it. Still the trespass is the same, recognized or unrecognized: and our ignorance, though it leaves us unconscious of evil, does not alter it.

And how solemn is the truth here taught us, that neither our conscience, nor our measure of light, nor our ability, but the truth of God, is the standard by which both sin and trespass are to be measured. *"Though he wist it not, yet is he guilty; he hath certainly trespassed against the Lord."* * If man's conscience or man's light were the standard, each man

* Chapter v. 17, 19.

might have a different rule. And, at this rate, right
or wrong, good or evil, would depend, not upon God's
truth, but on the creature's apprehension of it. At
this rate, the filthiest of unclean beasts could not be
convicted of uncleanness, while it could plead that it
had no apprehension of that which was pure and
seemly. But we do not judge thus in the things of
this world; neither does God judge so in the things
of heaven. Who argues that because swine are filthy,
therefore the standard of cleanliness is to be set by
their perceptions or ability; or that because they seem
unconscious of their state, therefore the distinction
between what is clean and unclean must be relinquished.
No: we judge not by their perceptions, but our own;
with our light and knowledge, not their ignorance, as
our standard. God, in like manner, though in grace
He finds means for pardoning it, still judges evil as
evil wherever He meets it. Our blindness does not
alter His judgment; for it is our sin and that alone
which has caused the blindness.

Such is trespass, and such the measure of it, a measure ever apparently widening according to our knowledge; for He who calls us, leads us to see as He sees,
not only His grace, but our own deep and constant
need of it. But, blessed be God, He that convinces of
sin, testifies of Him also by whose Offering sins are
pardoned. He that sees Jesus in the Trespass-offering,
sees trespass met; for Christ has confessed it, borne
its judgment, paid its penalty. Not only was "His
soul an offering *for sin*,"—in this we get the Sin-offer-

ing,—but "He was wounded *for our transgressions*," *
the judgment for trespass was also laid upon Him.
Here, as in the Sin-offering, He stood "the just for
the unjust," † confessing the wrongs of His people as
His wrongs ; and for those wrongs He made full
restitution ; and we in Him have satisfied God. All
this, however, is so nearly allied to the Sin-offering,
that I pass it as briefly as may be, to go on to those
particulars which are more definite, and specially characteristic of the Trespass-offering.

These are two. In the Trespass-offering, besides the
life laid down, the value of the trespass, according to
the priest's valuation of it, was paid in shekels of the
sanctuary, to the injured party. Then, in addition to
this, a fifth part more, in shekels also, was added to
the sum just spoken of, which, together with the amount
of the original wrong or trespass, was paid by the
trespasser to the person trespassed against. ‡ These
particulars, respecting the payment of money in connexion with the offering, are not only very definite, but
very remarkable. It may be well, therefore, before we
consider them separately, to note how distinctly all this
differed from the Sin-offering.

In the Sin-offering we see nothing of money : there
was no estimation by the priest, nor any fifth part
added. Indeed, from the nature of the case, there
could be neither of these, for they depend entirely
on the nature of trespass. In the Sin-offering the

* Compare Isaiah liii. 5, 10.   † 1 Pet. iii. 18.
‡ Chapter v. 15, 16, and vi. 5, 6.

offerer was a sinner: and his sin was met and judged in the victim. A perfect victim bore the penalty; a sinless one was judged for sin. In all this the one thought presented to us is sin receiving its rightful wages. We see due *judgment inflicted* on the sinner's substitute; and this having been inflicted, justice is satisfied. In the Trespass-offering, with the exception of "trespass" instead of "sin," we have all this precisely the same as in the Sin-offering. The victim's life is given for trespass: judgment is inflicted, and so far justice is satisfied. But in the Trespass-offering, there is *more than this,*—arising, as we shall see, out of the nature of trespass,—*the original wrong or evil is remedied; and further, a fifth part is added to it.* Observe, in the Trespass-offering the wrong inflicted is made up and restored by the offerer. According to the priest's valuation, the injured party receives his own, or the value of it, back again. Nor is this all; more than the original loss is repaid: the loss is more than remedied. These two most interesting particulars, specially characterizing, as they do, the atonement of the Trespass-offering, result directly and immediately from the distinction between sin and trespass. The apprehension of this distinction is absolutely necessary, if we would understand what remains of the Trespass-offering.

Sin then, I repeat, is the evil of our nature; and the offering for this, the Sin-offering, is for *what we are.* In the case of trespass, the offering is for *what we have done,* for actual wrong committed against some one.

Now, it follows from the distinct nature of these things, that the atonement or satisfaction for each must differ, in measure at least; for that which would fully satisfy justice in reference to sin, would by no means do so in reference to trespass. In the case of sin—that is, our sinful nature, where no actual robbery or wrong had been committed against any one—justice would be fully satisfied by the death and suffering of the sinner. But the mere suffering and death of the sinner would not make satisfaction for the wrong of trespass. For the victim merely to die for trespass, would leave the injured party a loser still. The trespasser indeed might be punished, but the wrong and injury would still remain. The trespasser's death would not repair the trespass, nor restore those rights which another had been robbed of. Yet, till this was done, atonement or satisfaction could scarcely be considered perfect. Accordingly, to make satisfaction in the Trespass-offering, there is not only judgment on the victim, but restitution also: the right of which another had been defrauded is satisfied; the wrong fully repaid.

To illustrate this. Suppose some noxious creature. *It is evil:* for this it merits death: the infliction of death would be judgment of the evil, and justice here could claim no more. But suppose this creature had also *done evil* and robbed us; its mere death will not repair the injury. Satisfaction for this will not be complete unless the injury done is made good in all points. In a word, atonement for trespass implies restitution; without this, though the trespasser is judged, the claim of trespass remains still unsatisfied. But in Christ man has made full satisfaction. God is not a loser even from the wrong of trespass. Nor this only. He receives even more. But let us look at the distinct particulars.

(3.) In the Trespass-offering we get restitution, full restitution for the original wrong. *The amount of the injury, according to the priest's valuation of it, is paid in shekels of the sanctuary to the injured person.** The thought here is not that trespass is punished, but that the injured party is repaid the wrong. The payment was in shekels: these "shekels of the sanctuary" were the appointed standard by which God's rights were measured ;† as it is said, " And all thy estimation shall be according to the shekel of the sanctuary."‡ Thus they represent the truest measure, God's standard by which He weighs all things. By this standard the trespass is weighed, and then the value paid to the injured person.

And God and man, though wronged by trespass, each receive as much again from man in Christ through the Trespass-offering. God was injured by trespass in His holy things, His rights unpaid, His claim slighted: for man was ofttimes a robber, taking for himself the fat or life, God's claim in the offerings. Thus, if I may so say, God through man was a loser: but at the

---

* Chapter v. 15.

† See Exodus xxx. 13, 24, xxxviii. 24, 25; Leviticus xxvii. 3, 25; Numbers iii. 47, 50, xviii. 16.

‡ Leviticus xxvii 25.

hands of Christ the loss has been repaid : and whatever was lost through man in the First Adam, has been made up to the full in the Second Adam. Whether honour, service, worship, or obedience, whatever God could claim, whatever man could rob Him of, all this has He received again from man in Christ, "according to the priest's estimation in shekels of the sanctuary."

But man also was injured by trespass ; and he, too, receives as much again. Christ for man as offerer of the Trespass-offering, must offer to injured man the value of the original injury. And such as accept His offering, find their loss through man's trespass more than paid. Has trespass wronged man of life, peace, or gladness, he may claim and receive through Christ repayment. For man to man, as for man to God, Christ stands the One in whom man's wrongs are remedied. The wrong done to God has been met. God clearly is no loser now by trespass. And the wrong done to man is no less paid for. Man need not, more than God, be a loser.

(4.) But this is not all. Not only is the original wrong paid, but a *fifth part more is paid with it* in the Trespass-offering.* Not only is the original claim, of which God and man had been wronged, satisfied : but something more, "a fifth," is added with it.

And first, what of the amount ? It is "*a fifth part.*" To find the import of this, we must again go back to Genesis. If I mistake not, the first place in Scripture where "the fifth" is mentioned, will lead us to appre-

* Chapter v. 16, vi. 5.

hend its import.   The particulars will be found in the
history of Joseph.   Briefly, the facts are these.   Before
the great seven years' famine, though Egypt was Pharaoh's land, and the Egyptians his people, yet both
were independent of him in some way which evidently
was not the case afterwards.   This we gather from the
fact that after the famine "a fifth," never paid before,
was paid to Pharaoh, in token that both land and people were Pharaoh's by another claim.   We read that
" when that year was ended, the Egyptians came to
Joseph the second year, and said unto him, We will
not hide it from my lord, how that our money is
spent ; my lord also hath our herds of cattle : there is
not ought left in the sight of my lord, but our bodies
and our lands : wherefore shall we die before thine
eyes, both we and our land ?   Buy us and our land for
bread, and we and our land will be servants unto
Pharaoh ; and give us seed, that we may live, and not die,
that the land be not desolate.   And Joseph bought all
the land of Egypt for Pharaoh ; for the Egyptians sold
every man his field, because the famine prevailed over
them : so the land became Pharaoh's.   Then Joseph
said unto the people, Behold, I have bought you this
day, and your land, for Pharaoh : lo, here is seed for
you, and ye shall sow the land.   And it shall come to
pass, in the increase, that ye shall give *the fifth part* to
Pharaoh, and four parts shall be your own.   And they
said, Thou hast saved our lives : let us find grace in the
sight of my lord, and we will be Pharaoh's servants.
And Joseph made it a law over the land of Egypt unto

this day, that Pharaoh should have *the fifth part;* except the land of the priests only, which became not Pharaoh's." *

We see here that "*the fifth part*" paid to Pharaoh, was the acknowledgment that all had been forfeited to him through misery. We learn, too, that in whatever way the Egyptians had been his people heretofore, they were now, through their need, made his by another claim. Accordingly, the payment of "a fifth" henceforward, wherever we meet with it in Scripture,† is the acknowledgment that the person paying it has lost and forfeited that whereof "the fifth" was offered. It is a witness not only that the sum or thing yielded up, has been yielded of necessity, as a debt, not as a free gift, but that the whole of that whereof the fifth was paid, was the right and property of him to whom its "fifth" was rendered. Thus its import in the Trespass-offering seals the character of the offering, testifying that what was given was indeed a debt, and not a free gift.‡

* Genesis xlvii. 18–26.

† It is only found in the law of the Trespass-offerings, Leviticus v. vi.; and in the law concerning vows or dedicated things, Leviticus xxvii. In both cases evidently the purport is the same.

‡ If I mistake not, this "*fifth*" is also connected with the tenth or *tithe;* the fifth being two tenths, or a double tithe. One tenth was paid by God's people before anything was forfeited in any way, as the acknowledgment that he to whom it was paid had a claim on all that of which a tenth was offered. But after a thing was forfeited by vow or trespass, (Lev. xxvii. and v. vi.,) we find that a fifth or double tithe was rendered. By the law in Exodus xxii. 4, 7, 9, any act of trespass gave him who had been trespassed against a double claim, or rather a claim to *double the amount of the original*

But while this was the import of giving "the fifth part," yet by the addition of this fifth the injured party became in truth a gainer. So far from losing by trespass, he received more back again: and this is what we have now to consider. Wonderful indeed are the ways of God: how unsearchable are His counsels and wisdom! Who would have thought that from the entrance of trespass, both God and man should in the end be gainers. But so it is. From man in Christ both God and man have received back more than they were robbed of. All things are indeed of God; yet it is from man in Christ, and this in consequence of trespass, that God, according to His wondrous purpose, receives back more than that of which sin had robbed Him. In this sense, " where sin abounded," yea, and because sin abounded, "grace did more abound." Just as in the case above alluded to, which I doubt not is typical, and typical, if I mistake not, of very kindred truth, the effect of the famine and misery on the Egyptians was to give Pharaoh a claim not possessed before; so the effect of the entrance of trespass has been to give the injured person, whether God or man, a claim on the person and property of the trespasser, which before trespass entered was all unknown.

I would to God this were more fully seen. We should then oftener hear of grace, of rights more sel-

wrong or injury inflicted on him. Thus when trespass had been committed and confessed, "the fifth" was paid as the acknowledgment of the double claim. But this only by the way, as marking, if I mistake not, the connexion between the "tithe" and the "fifth part."

dom: nor should we so often see Christians shrinking
from that which we call grace, but to the exercise of
which we are nevertheless most surely debtors. But to
explain this :—Before trespass entered, God only claimed
His part or right. He had a right to holy things as
His portion, and these He looked for from man. But
since trespass has entered, His claim is more: the
original right and the fifth part added. "The fifth"
was, as we have seen, the token how much had been
forfeited by the trespasser. Its payment testified that
he to whom it was given had now not only his original
right, but a still further claim upon him who wronged
him. Thus God's claim through trespass is greater:
and the same is true with regard to man's claim. Before trespass entered, man too had his claim : that claim
was his right, that claim was justice. But since trespass has entered, his claim is more: more than his
right is now his claim from the trespasser. The fact
that God has been wronged by man, and that Christ
stands for man confessing trespasses, gives God a claim
upon Him, not only for the original right, but for more
than the first claimed holy things. So, too, because
man has been injured by man, and because Christ
stands for man as his substitute, therefore man, injured
by trespass, has a claim on Christ, not for the original
right only, but for greater blessings.

And this claim Christ never refuses : nor are those
in Christ free to shrink from it. They, too, as "in
Him," are called, yea, and they are debtors, to deal in
grace far beyond the claim of justice. The world may

M

think that to mete out justice is the highest path of
which man is capable.   But Christ has shewn a higher
still ; and "he that abideth in Him is called to walk as
He walked."*   Such a path, of course, as every other
step after Christ, if followed, will surely cost us something.   But costly things become king's children : we
are rich enough to lose this world.   May the Lord
make His people know their calling, and conform them
to Him in grace even as in glory !   But I will not
pursue this here, as further on I must again touch it
in its bearing on the believer's walk.   I merely add
therefore,—"Christ set us an example :"† and He
yielded, not merely rights, but grace, to every man.

Thus much then, for what is specially characteristic
of the Trespass-offering, and as marking where it differs
from the other offerings.   It only remains to notice,

II. THE VARIETIES OR GRADES IN THIS OFFERING.
These are fewer than in any other offering, teaching us
that those who apprehend this aspect of Christ's work,
will apprehend it all very much alike.   Doubtless, the
cause of this lies in the nature of trespass, as it stands
distinct from sin.   It will be remembered, that in the
Sin-offering the varieties were most numerous, and that
because sin in us may be, and is, so differently apprehended ; but trespass, the act of wrong committed, if
seen at all, can scarce be seen differently.

Accordingly, we find but one small variety in the
Trespass-offering, for I can scarce regard the two different aspects of trespass as varieties.   These aspects are,

<hr>

* 1 John ii. 6.   † 1 Peter ii. 21.

first, trespasses against God,* and then trespasses against our neighbour ; † but this distinction is more like the difference between the offerings, than the varieties in the different grades of the same. It simply points out distinct bearings of trespass, for which in each case the atonement seen is precisely similar.

There is, however, one small yet remarkable difference between the two grades of the offering for wrongs in holy things. In the first grade, which gives us the fullest view of the offering, we read of the life laid down, the restitution made, and the fifth part added. But *in the lower class, the last of these is unnoticed: "the fifth part" is quite unseen.‡* And how true this is in the experience of Christians. Where the measure of apprehension is full, there not only the life laid down, and the restitution made in the Trespass-offering, but all the truth also which is taught in the "fifth part," will be seen as a consequence of trespass and a part of the Trespass-offering. Not so, however, where the apprehension is limited : here there is no addition seen beyond the amount of the original trespass.

But I hasten to conclude these Notes on the distinctive character of the Offerings. We have considered them separately; but we must never forget that though there are different aspects, there is but *One Offering.* Jesus, our blessed Lord, by His one oblation of Himself once offered for ever, has perfectly met, and perfectly satisfied,

* Chapter v. 15–19. † Chapter vi. 1–7.
‡ Compare verses 15, 16, which contain the higher grade, with verses 17, 18, which give the lower.

and that for us who believe, all that these emblems typify. I know that saints do not, and cannot see all the aspects of His Offering equally; but God sees all, and sees it "for us." In this surely we may rest. Blessed indeed is it so to grow in grace that we can "apprehend that for which we are apprehended:" but after all the joy is this, that we are indeed apprehended. And though our knowledge of what is Christ's and ours is still small, the day that is coming shall reveal it. Then when that which is perfect is come, our present knowledge, which is but in part, shall be done away. Blessed Lord, hasten Thy coming, to gladden with Thine own presence those whom Thou hast saved with Thy blood!

THE OFFERINGS AS A WHOLE.

1 PETER iv. 1.—ROMANS xii. 1, 2.

UNION with Christ is that which essentially constitutes a Christian. Nor is this union something changeful or visionary: it is a reality wrought by the Holy Ghost. The Church is "in Christ Jesus;"* and, as a consequence, "as He is, so are we in this world;"† identified with Him in His shame and in His joys; in His death, His burial, and His resurrection.‡

And truly the figures which are used to describe this union are such as we should never have dared to appropriate, had they not been given to us in our Father's Word, and were they not sealed in our hearts by His Spirit. What is the fellowship of brethren? What the union of the bridegroom and bride? What is the union of members with the head, of the branches with the vine, yea, of Christ with God; such is the union of saints with Christ, such the bond which binds us to Him. Not only does Christ say of His people,—"They

* Rom. xii. 5; 2 Cor. v. 17; Gal. i. 22; Eph. i. 3; 1 Thess. iv. 16; 1 John v. 20, &c., &c.
† 1 John iv. 17   ‡ Rom. vi. 4, 8; Col. ii. 12, iii. 1.

are not of the world, even as I am not of the world;"* but if He is "the Head," they are "the members," and both but "one body." "As the many members are one body, so also is Christ."† The context and argument here plainly demand that the sense should be, "so also is *the Church;*" but the Church and Christ "are not twain, but one:"‡ therefore the Apostle writes, "So also is Christ:" "For ye are the body of Christ, and members in particular." "And no man ever yet hated his own body; but nourisheth and cherisheth it, even as the Lord the Church: for we are members of His body, of His flesh, and of His bones."§

This union has its consequences, and they are most important, having reference to our standing and to our walk in Christ.

For the first of these, *our standing* in Christ, faith apprehends it: and thus we have peace with God. We see a man, "the man Christ Jesus," as man in perfectness standing "for us:" by His perfect sacrifice of Himself meeting God's claim on man, and thus in His person reconciling man to God. The sight of this, or rather the faith of it, gives peace. We see man reconciled to God through the blood of Jesus. His place, therefore, is now by faith apprehended as ours. Through Him, and in Him, by the Spirit, we claim and realize it.

But the union of Christ and His Church not only affects our standing; it must, if it be a reality, affect

---

* John xvii. 14, 16.   † 1 Cor. xii. 12.
‡ Eph. v. 31, 32.   § Eph. v. 29, 30.

our walk. It is true, indeed, that our walk, as being
part of our experience, and our experience being but
the measure of our apprehension, through our lack of
spiritual power, is constantly short of that for which
we are apprehended.* But our standard is still that
for which we are apprehended, and that is the walk of
Christ. "He that saith he abideth in Him, ought
himself also so to walk, even as He walked."† Indeed,
the work of the Spirit is but to verify *in* all Christ's
members that which is already true *for* them in the
person of their Head. To see, therefore, what is true
of Him as our Head, cannot be looked at alone in its
connexion with our standing. If we are Christ's, it
must necessarily take us further, leading us to know
what should be the measure of our walk, and teaching
us to judge in it, as unbecoming our calling, all that in
us is contrary to the walk of Christ. If it be true that
we are indeed His members, by the living Spirit bound
to Him, to be His for ever; if it be true that in Him
we are dead and risen, and if through grace we can
rejoice in this; we are only the more called on in the
knowledge of this to seek to be conformed to Him,
that so the things which are true for us in Him, may
be made true in our soul's experience by the Spirit.

Now, there are not a few who seem to see one part
of this truth, but who appear incapable of receiving
both parts; some exclusively pressing that which bears
upon our walk, others that which is connected with
our standing. The consequence inevitably is meagre-

* Phil. iii. 12.   † 1 John ii. 6.

ness in both, while the truth of God is on each point deformed and weakened. Those who, while they see the standard for our walk in Christ, do not see the believer's place in Him as accepted, uncertain of their place, while aiming to apprehend, lose the joy and strength which flows from knowing that they are apprehended. As a consequence, they lower the standard of their walk, seeking only just so much of the Spirit's fruits as will prove them Christians. Others again, having read of Christ's oneness with His Church, and as a consequence the believer's acceptance in Him, seem often by no means equally to understand the necessary connexion of this with their walk as Christians. Such profess to see their union with Christ, that He died for them, that they died in Him, without seeing that this union, if indeed it be real, must involve their daily dying with Him. Indeed, the very reverse of this is practically asserted. They seem to think Christ died in the flesh, that they might live in it. With such the doctrine really is this,—Christ died to sin that I might live to sin. I ask, is there anything like this to be found within the whole compass of Scripture? Such a doctrine exhibited as it is in the lives of hundreds, though practically denying our union with Christ, because so often stated by those who profess to know that union, has done more than ought else to hide it. The humble soul, shrinking from the thought of making Christ's love to us an indulgence or apology for sin, recoils instinctively from that which, while it speaks of union with Christ, in works utterly denies it.

To connect this with THE OFFERINGS. The Offerings set forth Christ. We see in them how man in Christ has made atonement. Our *standing* as believers immediately flows from this: for "as He is, so are we in this world." We look at the Sin and Trespass-offerings, and see that the sin of man has been fully borne. We look at the Burnt and Meat-offerings, and see all God's requirements satisfied. And this is our confidence, that as Christ "for us" has been without the camp, as "for us" He has been laid on the altar; so truly do we, if quickened by His Spirit, stand in Him, even as He is: "for by one offering He hath perfected for ever them that are sanctified." *

But there is also the other aspect of this truth. We are one with Christ: therefore we should *walk* even as He walked. In this view His Offering, as our example, sets before us the model and standard for our self-sacrifice. And just as Christ's sacrifice for us had varied aspects, as satisfying God, as satisfying man, as bearing sin; so, though of course in a lower sense, will our self-sacrifice, just as it is conformed to His, and because we are one with Him, have these same aspects. It is in this way that, in a secondary sense, the Typical offerings have an application to Christians. Thus we also are offerers and our bodies offerings; as it is written, "Present your bodies a living sacrifice."† Not indeed

* Heb. x. 14.   † Rom. xii. 1.

as though by our self-sacrifice we could make Christ's Offering for us more acceptable :—" We are sanctified by the offering of His body once for all ;"* "we are made accepted in the Beloved :"†—but as the consequence of our acceptance in Him, and as the fruit of our union with Him through the Spirit. Therefore we offer ; and as already accepted in Christ, though in ourselves poor, weak, and worthless, our sacrifices, whether our works or person, as the fruits of Christ's Spirit, are acceptable through Him. Of course there is in His pure Offering that which will find no counterpart in us. Dissimilarities neither few nor small arise from the fact that He was sinless, we sinners. Yet the saint, as in spirit alive with Christ, as entering into His willing mind,‡ yea, as already one with Him, as in Him dead and risen, will seek further "to be made conformable to His death."§ His self-sacrifice may fail in many ways : but his rule is the offering of the body of Jesus Christ.

I proceed therefore to trace, in conclusion, how far the various aspects of the offering of the body of Christ, may be applicable to those who, being members of His mystical body, are called to walk even as He walked.

I. And first THE BURNT-OFFERING. This was man satisfying God : man in Christ *giving himself to God as His portion*. We have seen how *for us* this was fulfilled in Christ. We inquire how far *in us* it may be fulfilled by the Spirit. And in this light, both in its

* Heb. x. 10.   † Eph. i. 6.
‡ 1 Cor. ii. 16.   § Phil. iii. 10

measure and character, the Burnt-offering stands a witness how we should "yield ourselves."* First, as to *its measure.* It was "wholly burnt." No part was withheld from God. Can we mistake this teaching? Does it not plainly say that conformity to Christ must cost us something,—yea, that it involves entire self-surrender, even though that surrender lead us to the cross? "I will not," said David, "offer unto the Lord a Burnt-offering of that which doth cost me nothing."† The Burnt-offering is still costly, befitting Him who receives it at our hands. The Burnt-offering was God's claim; that claim was love; as He said, "Thou shalt love the Lord with all thine heart." The fulfilment of this required a life from Christ. It will demand our lives just in measure as we walk with Him. "For love is strong as death; jealousy is cruel as the grave; the coals thereof are coals of fire, which hath a most vehement flame."‡

And in these days when pious worldliness is so successfully misusing the truth of God;—when, in the light of the advanced wisdom of this our age, self-sacrifice is exploded folly;—when the mere fact that a path involves loss in this world, is considered a good reason for our at once avoiding it;—when the doctrine of the cross, as it bears upon our walk, is not only omitted, but openly condemned;—when to give up the world is injudiciousness, and to crucify the flesh a return to law;—in such days we do well to look at the Burnt-offering, as setting before us the example we are called to follow. Alas! that it should be so, but it is

* Rom. vi. 13.   † 2 Sam. xxiv. 24.   ‡ Canticles viii. 6.

not denied, by some it is even gloried in, that Christianity now involves no loss; the times are altered: the world is changed. The offence of the cross has ceased: they that live godly need not suffer.* A path has been found, a happy path some think it, wherein the highest profession of Christ costs nothing; nay, in which such a profession, so far from involving the loss of this world, is the surest way to gain its praise. According to this doctrine, Christ suffered for us; apostles, prophets, martyrs, all suffered. They, in their pilgrimage, lost this world for another; but we, in happier days, can possess both worlds. It cannot be. If God's Word be true, our path after Christ must be still a sacrifice. We, as they of old, if followers of Christ, must with Him "present our bodies a living sacrifice."†

And indeed if we do but weigh these words,— "Present your bodies a living sacrifice,"—we cannot shut our eyes to what is involved in them, and that we are called to give up ourselves. Can we do this without cost, or without feeling that sacrifice is indeed sacrifice, though it be willing sacrifice? Impossible. Christ felt His sacrifice: and so surely shall we, if we offer with Him. Nor shall we grudge this. Just as it was His joy to give Himself; as He said, "I delight to do Thy will, O God;"‡ so in us also, as quickened with Him, "the spirit is willing, though the flesh is weak."§

I do not wish to press every detail of the Burnt-

* See 2 Tim. iii. 12.   † Rom. xii. 1.
‡ Psalm xi. 8.   § Matt. xxvi. 41.

offering in its application to our individual walk; yet
the general character of the victim may be a guide to
the character, as its entire surrender was to *the measure*,
of our offering.   We saw, in the application of the type
to Christ, how its varieties of bullock, lamb, and turtle-
dove, each brought out some distinct particular in the
character of our blessed Lord.   In each of these we
have an example we can comprehend, however far we
may be from attaining to it.   Would to God that in
active yet patient service, in silent unmurmuring submission, in gentleness and innocency of life, we might
be conformed to Him who went before us.   These
emblems of His offering, if they mean anything,
sufficiently shew us,—even as His example shewed it,
—that self-sacrifice is not to make us great in this
world: service, submission, meekness, will gain no
crown here.   We cannot be heroes in this world, if we
offer ourselves to God in the character these emblems
typify.   But if conformed to them, we shall be more
like Christ.   May He give us grace gladly to acquiesce
in the likeness!   He, as man in a proud and violent
world, yea, and for us, was all that these emblems
typify.   He bore the cross such a character involved;
He shrunk not from the reproach it brought Him.
He was despised and rejected of men, as a lamb slain,
and none to pity.   In a word, and this is indeed the
sum of it, He was content to be nothing, that God
might be all.   May the corresponding reality be more
manifested in us, through subjection to the power of
His indwelling Spirit.

II. But let us pass on to the MEAT-OFFERING. Here, as man for men, Christ offered Himself as the fruit of the earth, that is, *as man's meat.* In doing this, He gave Himself to God, yet with special reference to man, and as meeting man's claim on Him. Man had a claim upon man ; God had ratified the claim, saying, "Thou shalt love thy neighbour as thyself." In the Meat-offering, Christ met and satisfied this claim, by giving Himself to God as man's portion. Let us, in the light of His sacrifice, learn how far His members, though but " leavened bread," may yield themselves to God as man's meat.

To turn then to our Pattern. What, as meeting man's claim, was the character of His Offering, and what the measure of it ? For *its character,* " the bruised corn," " the oil," " the salt," and " the frankincense," are sufficiently explicit. For *the measure* of it, it is enough to say, the Type shews us the whole consumed. Such is our standard. Its import we cannot mistake. The question is, How far we may be conformed to it ? To answer this let us look to other days, and see how far poor sinful man has been conformed to it. Time was when the Church, though but " a leavened cake,"* was so far filled with the anointing of the Holy Ghost, that "the multitude of them which believed were of one heart and of one soul : neither said any of them that ought of the things which he possessed was his own ; but they had all things common. Neither was there any that lacked : for as many as were possessors of

* Lev. xxiii. 17.

lands or houses sold them, and brought the prices of the things that were sold, and laid them down at the apostles' feet; and distribution was made to every man according as he had need." * Here was a Meat-offering, and a costly one: but costly as it was, it was not then a rare one. In that day there were living men, who for the gospel had "lost all things," † who yet, while suffering this, were willing to suffer more, even to give their own lives to God for others. "Yea," says Paul, "if I be poured out," (he alludes to the Drink-offering which was offered as an adjunct to the Meat-offering‡) — "Yea if I be poured out on the sacrifice and service of your faith, I joy and rejoice with you." § Nor was he alone in this. Time would fail to tell of others, Onesiphorus, Epaphroditus, Philemon, Phebe, who "oft refreshed the bowels of the saints." || Their lives were indeed a Meat-offering.

There is yet a Church. There must yet be offerings; and thank God we yet hear of sacrifices. But what is their measure, what their character? How far are they conformed to those we have but just spoken of? Let each here judge himself. This only will I say, that just in measure as we are like our Master,—just in proportion as we accept His words as the rule for the measure, as well as the manner of our sacrifice,—just so far as in the steps of those of old, we "sell that we have, and give alms,"—just as we "give to him that asketh of us, and from him that would borrow of us

* Acts iv. 32–35.   † Phil. iii. 8.   ‡ Numbers xv. 1–12.
§ Phil. ii. 17. || Philemon 7.

turn not away,"—just so far shall we find our path a sacrifice, involving not only cost, but unexpected trial. As of old, so is it now. The box of alabaster, of ointment, of spikenard very precious, cannot be poured upon the head of Christ, without exciting the anger of those who see it. Even disciples must complain. "When the disciples saw it, they had indignation, saying, To what purpose was this waste?" Even so is it now. Self-sacrifice is still reproved, even by those who follow the Crucified One. With not a few, such a course is sufficient proof of the lack of common sense or common prudence in the person guilty of it. But what saith the Lord? "When Jesus understood it, He said unto them, Why trouble ye the woman? for she hath wrought a good work upon me: for in that she hath poured this ointment on my body, she did it for my burial. Verily I say unto you, Wheresoever this gospel shall be preached, there shall also this, that this woman hath done, be told for a memorial of her."* And in that coming day, when the gospel shall have done its work, in gathering a people out of all nations, when the Son of man shall come in His glory, and all the holy angels with Him,—in that day when the righteous answer, When saw we Thee an hungered, and fed Thee, the King shall say, Inasmuch as ye did it to my brethren, ye did it unto me.

III. I pass on to THE PEACE-OFFERING. This was that view of the Offering which shewed us *the Offerer fed.* In the Peace-offering, the offerer, with the Priest,

* Matt. xxvi. 7–13.

and God, partook of, that is, found satisfaction in, the
offering.   Can it be said that in this aspect of the
Offering, our self-sacrifice can at all resemble Christ's?
Can our poor offerings yield any satisfaction to ourselves?   Can they afford any satisfaction to Christ and
God?   I must take heed what I say here.   But what
saith the Lord?   Let His Word in each case supply
the answer.   That answer will teach us that in this
aspect also the Peace-offering has a fulfilment, not only
in Christ, but in His members.

And first, for God's part.   Does God find satisfaction
in our offerings?   The following witness is sufficiently
clear:—"To do good and to communicate forget not:
for with such sacrifices God is well pleased."*   So
again, the offering sent by the Philippians to Paul was
"a sweet savour:" God found in it something pleasant
to Him:—"The things which were sent from you, *are
an odour of a sweet smell, a sacrifice acceptable, well-
pleasing to God.*"†   The words here used in the original are the very same as those which the Septuagint
have used to express "a sweet savour" in the Peace-
offering.‡   What stronger proof can we need of God's
satisfaction in, and the value He puts upon, the offerings
of His Church.   "God loveth a cheerful giver;"§ and
as our greatest gift is "to give ourselves,"‖ so the
presentation of our bodies as living sacrifices is "ac-

---

* Heb. xiii. 16.   † Phil. iv. 18.
‡ St Paul's words are ὀσμὴ εὐωδίας τῷ θεῷ.   In the Peace
offering the Septuagint version gives ὀσμὴ εὐωδίας τῷ κυρίῳ.
§ 2 Cor. ix. 7.   ‖ 2 Cor. viii. 5.

ceptable unto the Lord."* And we need to remember this. It is possible, nay, it is easy, in our zeal against the doctrine of salvation by works, to leave the impression that all works are useless, none acceptable to God, or accepted of Him. I fear there are not a few who, practically at least, are in error upon this very question. The works of the flesh are indeed dead works; but the fruits of the Spirit, as they flow from Christ, as they are the witnesses of His grace, an offering to His praise, so do they come up before God through Him "a sweet savour."

But the Priest also fed in the Peace-offering. For the joy which our Priest finds in our offerings, poor and feeble though they be, it is enough to know, that even in the cup of cold water, in the bread to the hungry, He is refreshed and fed. "I was an hungered, *and ye gave me meat:* I was thirsty, *and ye gave me drink.*"† Oh, did we but know His joy in seeing us yield ourselves an offering for Him, to find that in a world which hated Him some remember Him while still away:—if we but realized the gladness of His soul in some work of faith or labour of love, forgotten it may be by the feeble doer, but treasured in the book of Him who is "not forgetful;"—we could not, I think, give up ourselves with such narrow, selfish, grudging hearts. Could we, if in our services to the poor we saw Christ in them, and realized that He received our gifts, present them with such niggard hands? Would not our best be freely offered Him?

* Rom. xii. 1.   † Matt. xxv. 35.

Suppose Him wanting bread. If we knew He lacked, that He was hungry, naked, sick, or suffering; would not our last shilling, our most precious time, be freely given to minister to Him? We can do so still. "I was sick, and ye visited me: I was a stranger, and ye took me in. Verily I say, Inasmuch as ye did it to my brethren, ye did it unto me."*

But further, the Peace-offering fed the offerer. And surely we have been strangers to self-sacrifice, if we need be told the joy it imparts to him who sacrifices. But what saith the Word? Paul, speaking of his service, says, "Yea, if I be sacrificed, *I joy, and rejoice with you.*"† So again to the Colossians, "*I rejoice* in my sufferings for you, and fill up that which is behind of the afflictions of Christ."‡ So again, "I count not my life dear unto me, so that I might finish my course *with joy.*"§ Not only is it true, that *for* our service "every one shall receive his own reward, according to his own labour;"‖ but *in* our service, in yielding ourselves to God, there is present joy with which a stranger intermeddleth not. "It is more blessed to give than to receive;"¶ and he who gives himself to God shall know this blessedness. "Sorrowful" he may be, "yet always rejoicing; poor, yet making many rich."** The very costliness of the sacrifice increases our joy, when we know that He, to whom we offer, rejoices with us.

IV. Thus far we have only followed the sweet-savour offerings, in their application to the Christian's walk.

* Matt. xxv. 40. † Phil. ii. 17. ‡ Col. i. 24. § Acts xx. 24.
‖ 1 Cor. iii. 8. ¶ Acts xx. 35. ** 2 Cor. vi. 10.

Are the remaining offerings, THE SIN and TRESPASS-
OFFERINGS, equally applicable to us upon this same
principle? I believe they are; though, as in the
preceding offerings, only applicable in a secondary way.
God forbid I should be mistaken upon this point, as
though I thought that the saint could atone for himself
or others. In this sense, any interference with the
Sin-offering would be a setting aside of the work of
Christ. Still, there is a sense and measure in which
the Sin-offering has its counterpart in us, as bearing on
our self-sacrifice : there is a sense in which the Christian
may bear sin, and suffer its judgment in his mortal
flesh. Just as the Burnt-offering,—which, in its first
and full application, shews Christ in perfectness once
offering Himself for man; by that One Oblation of
Himself once offered, meeting God's claim on man, and
so reconciling us to God for ever;—just as this Burnt-
offering, while as offered for us it secures our acceptance,
has also, as an example to us, an application to o
walk, shewing how man in Christ should offer himself,
through the Spirit giving himself to God; just so is
it in the Sin and Trespass-offerings. Without in the
least degree interfering with the atonement perfected
by the One great Sin-offering ;—while holding that by
that One perfect sacrifice, and by that alone, sin can
ever be purged; as it is written, "He by Himself
purged our sins;"* and again, "He hath put away sin
by the sacrifice of Himself ;"†—there is still a sense
in which the Christian, in offering himself to God, can

* Heb. i. 3.   † Heb. ix. 26.

and should use the Sin-offering, as well as the Burnt-offering, as his pattern. For lack of knowing this many are sparing that flesh, which the cross of Christ was given to crucify.

What then was THE SIN-OFFERING? It was that peculiar offering, in which the victim bore sin, and died for it. The question is, how far, even if at all, this is applicable to the Christian's offering. Is there anything to be wrought in us by the Spirit, answering to the dying for sin of the Sin-offering? Let the Scripture answer: "Christ hath once suffered for sins, the just for the unjust, that He might bring us to God, being put to death in the flesh, but quickened by the Spirit."* And what is the inference? Is it that the death of Christ is the reprieve to the flesh, its release from suffering? On the contrary, Christ's death in the flesh for sin is made our example: we too must also, yea therefore, die with Him. So it follows :—"Forasmuch then as Christ hath suffered for us in the flesh, arm yourselves likewise with the same mind: for he that hath suffered in the flesh hath ceased from sin."† The saint, as having been judged in the person of Christ, and knowing that for him Christ has borne the cross, follows on by that cross to judge and mortify all that he finds in himself still contrary to his Lord. The flesh in him is contrary to that Holy One: the flesh in him therefore must die. And instead of making Christ's cross the reprieve for that flesh, the child of God will use that cross to slay it. Others may

* 1 Peter iii. 18.   † 1 Peter iv. 1.

preach the cross of Christ as an excuse for carnal **and**
careless walking. He who abides in God's presence
will surely learn there that by the cross we must be
crucified with Christ. If he says, "God forbid that I
should glory, save in the cross of our Lord Jesus
Christ," he will add at once, "by whom the world is
crucified unto me, and I unto the world."*   I know
indeed that "there are enemies of the cross, whose God
is their belly, who glory in their shame ;"† who are
using the doctrine of the cross, to spare that flesh
which the cross should crucify. But God's truth is, that
so far from "the flesh" or "old man" being saved
from death by the cross, it is by it devoted to death and
to be crucified ; and that Christ's death, instead of being
a kind of indulgence for sin, or a reprieve of the life of
the flesh, the life of the old man, is to His members the
seal that their flesh must die, and that sin with its lusts
and affections must be mortified.‡

The fact is that the child of God, who, through ignorance of God's mind, or disobedience, instead of judging
the old man with his works, makes provision to fulfil

* Gal. vi. 14.   † Phil. iii. 19.

‡ It was but lately that in looking over a work just published, I
found the following objection to the doctrines of grace; that, "if
death be the penalty of sin, and Christ in dying for His people indeed bore the punishment due to them, how comes it that any
believers die?" Full well has the so-called Evangelical preaching
of the day merited such a rebuke—a rebuke which could never have
been heard, had the full truth of the cross been stated, namely,
that Christ's death is the witness to His people, that, since they are
His members, they must also be crucified with Him. See Rom. vi.;
Gal. ii. ; 1 Pet. iv.

the lusts thereof; such a one, if indeed he be Christ's, by not judging himself, only brings upon himself God's judgment. Happy they who, in communion with the Lord, learn and judge the flesh there, rather than in chastenings from Him. "If we would judge ourselves, we should not be judged of the Lord."* But if we reject this path : still the flesh must die. If we do not mortify it, God most surely will. "They that are Christ's have crucified the flesh."† "Our old man is crucified with Him."‡ And just as, because we are alive in Christ, we can, as risen with Him, yield our-selves to God, in spirit giving Him the fruits of right-eousness, a sweet savour to Him by Jesus Christ; so may we also, as one with Christ in the power and energy of the same Spirit, mortify our members which are upon the earth, and yield our flesh to death, to be crucified with Him.

How full, then, of teaching is the Sin-offering, viewed even in this lower light, merely as an example to us ! How does it seal that truth we are so slow to learn, that the flesh, the old man, must be judged and morti-fied ! I ask, how is this aspect of Christ's Offering, and our offering with Him, apprehended by Christians ? Another has said,—"The boast of our day is that Christ crucified is preached. But is He, even in this one respect, *fully* preached, or the doctrine of the cross fully apprehended ? Let the walk of those who make the boast answer. It is not insinuated that such are chargeable with licentiousness or immorality. But

* 1 Cor. xi. 31.   † Gal. v. 24.   ‡ Rom. vi. 6.

are they, therefore, not chargeable with 'walking after the flesh,' and 'making provision to fulfil its desires?' In the multitude of particulars it is difficult to make a selection. But what then is the high regard in which blood, and ancestry, and family connexion, are held by some? What is the regard to personal appearance and dress, in others? What the attention to ease and comfort, and often-times profuse expenditure, (not to speak of actual luxuries,) in the arrangement of the houses, tables, &c., of almost all? What are the accomplishments, on the acquiring of which so much time and money are spent? What the character of the education which most Christians, in common with the world, give their children? Or, to take a wider view still of making 'provision for the flesh,' apart from what is generally considered evil or sinful,—to what are all the discoveries in science, all the improvements in art, directed? What is the end of most of the trades and businesses followed in a professing Christian country, and often by Christians? Is all this, and a thousand other things too numerous to particularize, consistent with reckoning ourselves *dead* as to the old or natural man? Is this what the Scriptures intend by *crucifixion of the flesh?* Alas! full well do many of the professing Christians of our day shew that they are but half taught the very doctrine in which they make their boast; that they have but half-learned the lesson which even the cross teaches. They have learned that Christ was crucified *for them,* but they have not learned

that they are to be 'crucified *with Him ;*' or they have
found an explanation for this latter expression in the
imputation of His death for our justification ;—a part
of the truth, but not the whole; for in vain in this
explanation of the words should we seek an answer to
the objection which the Apostle anticipated. Yea,
rather, that objection is confirmed by it, for it is
nothing else than making the cross the reprieve of
the flesh from death. And then when death itself
comes to give the refutation to this creed, and to shew
that the Christian is not saved in the flesh, *then* is the
effect of this half-learned lesson seen. For, instead of
welcoming death as that of which his life has been the
anticipation, the execution of that sentence on the flesh,
which, since he has known Christ as crucified for him,
he has learned in its desert, and has been continually
passing on it in mind and spirit, the dying with Christ
daily, the 'being planted in the likeness of His death,'—
instead of being enabled in this view actually to glory
in his infirmities, in the weakness, yea, and the dissolu-
tion of the flesh, and like the victim found on the
arrival of his executioner to have anticipated the end
meditated for him, being found of death dead,—he is
scarcely resigned to die, and impatient of suffering in
the flesh. And why? Because that truth which the
Cross of Christ was designed to teach, he never distinctly understood, or rather experienced, namely, that
salvation is not in the flesh, but in the Spirit ; not
from death, but *out of* it; not the reinstating of the

old nature, but the conferring of a new, by the dying
and rising again with Christ."*

V. It only remains for us to look at THE TRESPASS-
OFFERING, in its bearing on the walk of saints. This
was that offering in which *restitution was made for
wrong;* the original claim with the added "fifth" was
paid by the trespasser. We have seen how this was
fulfilled for us in Christ, how at His hands God re-
covered all whereof man had robbed Him. We have
seen the consequence of this to those in Christ, how
they are complete in Him through whom we have
received the atonement. Our present inquiry is, how
this offering should affect our walk; how far our union
with Christ will make this view of His sacrifice an
example to us?

And first we have *restitution* here. Christ standing
for man makes full restitution for man's wrong and
trespass; "not with corruptible things, as silver and
gold;" † but by the value of His own Offering He
repays our trespass. In this sense we can make no
restitution. If Christ has not made it, we are lost.
The rest of our lives, if wholly spent for God, could
never atone for our acts of trespass. Each day would
bring its own proper claim. Works of supererogation,
therefore, we could have none. Yet there is a measure
and a sense in which the saint in fellowship with Christ

* Burgh's Tracts, "*On preaching Christ.*" Christ in His death.
Pp. 5, 6.
† 1 Pet. i. 18, 19.

will make restitution. Not indeed as to win acceptance, but as shewing how, according to his measure, through the Spirit, he sympathizes with Christ. As he has in days past, as the servant of sin, robbed man and God of their rights, so now, as having been made free from sin, he becomes the servant of righteousness. "Now, being made free from sin, and become servants to God, ye have your fruit unto holiness, and the end everlasting life." *

But there was *a fifth part added.* God or man, if wronged by trespass, not only received back their original claim. In consequence of trespass, more than that claim was due to them, the payment of which with a life, constituted the Trespass-offering. Under the law, God and man had each their claim on man: the measure of that claim, by God's own appointment, was righteousness: if man dealt justly toward God and man, nothing further than the right, nothing like grace, could by law be claimed of him. But it was different after he had trespassed. Then, by God's own appointment, right was no longer the measure of his debt to others. If we were sinless, we should without doubt be safe, yea, we might bring the law to justify us, in dealing mere rights to every one. But if the Old and New Testaments mean anything by what they teach on this point, the trespasser is the wrong man to contend for rights. The fact of our being trespassers gives God a claim upon us, not merely the original

* Rom. vi. 22.

claim, not the bare claim of right. Above and beside
this, the trespasser is a debtor to yield that which, but
for his being a trespasser, could never have been
claimed from him. I know we call this, dealing in
grace, to yield to sinners more than their just claim on
us. In a sense it is grace: it would be so fully, if we
ourselves were sinless before God. But because we are
convicted trespassers, and trespassers who make our
boast in grace, we are called, as the very witness of that
grace and of our need of it, to deal in what we call
grace to others. "Ye have heard that it hath been
said, An eye for an eye : but I say unto you, resist not
evil. Do good to them that hate you ; pray for them
that despitefully use you, and persecute you." * "And
when ye stand praying, forgive, if ye have ought against
any ; that your Father also which is in heaven may
forgive you your trespasses. But if ye do not forgive,
neither will your heavenly father forgive you your trespasses."† "For if ye love them that love you, what
thank have ye ? for sinners also love those that love
them. And if ye do good to them that do good to
you, what thank have ye ? for sinners also do even the
same. And if ye lend to them of whom ye hope to
receive, what thank have ye ? for sinners also lend to
sinners, to receive as much again. But love your
enemies, and do good, and lend, hoping for nothing
again ; and ye shall be the children of the Highest : for
He is kind to the unthankful and to the evil."‡

* Matt. v. 38-44.   † Mark xi. 25, 26.   ‡ Luke vi. 32-35.

This is very plain. But how far is it acted upon by many who profess to be one with Christ? Provided we have been *just*, who asks, have I been *gracious*, in my dealings to my fellow-men? Who scruples to go to law,* who fears to claim his rights, little thinking of the added "fifth" of the Trespass-offering? And who, were his rights withheld by law, would hesitate to strive against the law by political agitation or otherwise; forgetting that grace, not right, must be the law, as it is the hope, of the trespasser? But I forbear upon this head. He that cannot hear Christ, will scarcely hear His feeble servant. "If they believe not Moses and the prophets, neither will they be persuaded though one rose from the dead."

Such is "THE LAW OF THE OFFERINGS." It gives but one view of Christ: yet how much is involved in it, both as to our walk and standing. Do we not need this truth? Surely if ever there was a time when the truths connected with Christ's sacrifice were needed, that time is the present. As in the days of Christ, so now God's truth is used as the prop of error. Just as then the Law, which was given to prove man's sinfulness, was used by Pharisees to exalt man's righteousness; so now the Gospel, which was given to lead us to another world, is being used to make this world a more sure abiding place. I speak what is notorious: it is the boast of our age, that Christianity is doing what it

* 1 Cor. vi. 1, 7.

never did before.   It is giving temperance to the world
and peace to the nations, it is vindicating the liberty of
the slave; in a word, it is making for man a better
home, a safer resting-place, on this side the grave.
And all the while the world is still the world, and the
slave still, as before, the slave of lust.   Time was when
Christians gave up the world.   They now can mend it :
they need not leave it.   Oh, cunning device of the Evil
One, too easily followed by a deluded age!   God's truth
now, instead of laying man in his grave, with the certain hope of a resurrection morning, is used on all
hands, misused I should say, to perfect man in the
flesh, almost to deify him ;—used to prop "the things
which must be shaken," instead of leading us to those
"which cannot be moved,"—used to give an inheritance on this side death, instead of in the glory which
shall be revealed.   Oh, how does THE OFFERING judge
all this !   It speaks of sacrifice, even to the cross.   It
tells us that, as one with Christ, our portion in Him
must yet be His portion.   What had He here ?   He
suffered under Pontius Pilate ; He was crucified,
dead, and buried ; He rose again the third day ; He
ascended up into heaven ; He sitteth at the right hand
of God ; He shall come again to judge the quick and
dead.   What had He here ?   Nothing.   He took not as
His home a world unpurged by fire, a creation still under
the curse.   He passed through it as a rejected pilgrim.
We, too, if we would be like Him, must do so still.
As Luther said, " Our spouse is a bloody husband to

us." He will not let us have this world till He has it. His day is at hand : for that day He waits.* Let us be content, "yet a little while," to wait with Him. And while many are anticipating His kingdom, in a kingdom without His presence, and without His saints, let us look for the resurrection of the dead, and the life of the world to come.

* Heb. x. 13.

APPENDIX.

THE principle on which I have interpreted the Varieties of the Offerings is one which appears to lie open to an objection. My principle, it will be remembered, is that the Varieties in the Typical Offerings represent different aspects or apprehensions of Christ's One Offering: the different offerings giving us different aspects of His Offering; the different grades the various apprehensions of some one aspect.

In the preceding pages* I have briefly given the grounds for this judgment. An objection, however, may be made. It may be urged, that it is far more reasonable to suppose that God in His Word would give us representations of realities themselves rather than of certain apprehensions of them, inasmuch as since different apprehensions must be more or less imperfect, the representation of such in His Word would make that Word imperfect likewise.

The plausibility of this objection makes me notice it here. It is, however, I am convinced, unsound; proceeding throughout on an assumption opposed to reason and all experience. That this assumption is not sooner de-

Pages 40–47.

O

tected arises from the fact that it involves questions with which but few are conversant. The objection assumes, without appearing to assume anything, certain points connected with the capabilities of our perceptive faculties. The mass of mankind are content to use their perceptive faculties without ever troubling themselves to inquire what it is those faculties deal with. Any assumption, therefore, on such subjects, takes them into an unknown sphere, where, from misapprehension of what they seem to see, their most logical conclusions, because founded on misapprehension, may, and indeed necessarily must, be most irrational.

I say the objection makes assumptions. It does so on the subject of representations, assuming it reasonable to suppose that representations must be of realities rather than of certain apprehensions of realities. To this I say at once, that such a supposition, so far from being reasonable, is most unreasonable. For, first, it is acknowledged that the perceptive faculty, whether of things inward or outward, deals not with realities themselves, but only with their phenomena; which phenomena, though they pre-suppose the existence of realities, are not realities, but, as the name imports, only certain appearances of them. And secondly, it is equally plain, that pictures or similar representations, (and the types are confessedly such representations,) can of necessity be conversant with phenomena only, inasmuch as they only describe or represent what the perceptive faculty takes cognizance of. It follows hence at once, that if the Types are to represent what our perceptive faculties take cognizance of, they will necessarily be representations, not of realities themselves, but of certain appearances or apprehensions of them.

I am more and more satisfied that what we see of Christ and God, though true as far as it goes, (and surely most true it is,) is yet very far short of the ineffable reality "which passeth all understanding." Certain forms of the truth we have got: the reality, who has yet attained to know it?

THE END.

Printed in the United States of America

THISELTON MARK, D. Lit.

The Pedagogics of Preaching

A Short Essay in Practical Homiletics. Net

Much has been done for the Teacher in showing him the practical application in his work of the findings of the new Psychology, but comparatively little has been done in the field of "Psychology and Preaching." This scholarly and yet popular book applies to the art of preaching methods which have long been followed in the training of teachers.

FRANK W. GUNSAULUS, D.D.

The Minister and The Spiritual Life

Yale Lectures on Preaching for 1911. Net $1.25.

Among the phases of this vital subject treated by the pastor of The Central Church, Chicago, are: The Spiritual Life and Its Expression in and Through Ministering; The Spiritual Life in View of Changes in Philosophical and Theological View-Points; The Spiritual Life in Its Relation to Truth and Orthodoxy; The Spiritual Life and Present Social Problems, etc.

PROF. A. T. ROBERTSON, D.D.

The Glory of the Ministry

Paul's Exultation in Preaching. Cloth, net $1.25.

Rev. F. B. Meyer says: "I think it is the best of all your many books and that is saying a good deal. Its illuminating references to the Greek text, its graphic portraiture of the great Apostle, its allusions to recent literature and current events, its pointed and helpful instructions to the ministry combine to give it very special value."

SAMUEL CHARLES BLACK, D.D.

Building a Working Church

12mo, cloth, net $1.25.

Every pastor or church officer no matter how successful he may be, will find practical, vital suggestions for strengthening some weak place in his present organization. The author makes every chapter bear directly upon some specific phase of the church building problem.

WILLIAM E. BARTON, D. D.

Rules of Order for Religious Assemblies

8mo, cloth, net 50c.

This work is entirely undenominational and will be found adapted to use in any religious assembly whether church, council, association or convention.

CORTLAND MYERS, D. D.

Real Prayer

12mo, cloth, net 50c.

"Dr. Myers' purpose in writing this book is to make real the power which comes from the habit of prayer. The reality of this dynamic spiritual force is clearly set forth in chapters on the Real Power, the Real Presence, the Real Purity, the Real Plea, the Real Persistence and the Real Purpose of Prayer."—*Service.*

HENRY C. MABIE, D. D.

The Divine Reason of the Cross

A Study of the Atonement as the Rationale of Our Universe. 12mo, cloth, net $1.00.

Principal P. T. Forsyth of Hackney College, London, says: "I have found the book very suggestive. I wish the view you promote might get more hold to deepen religion and save it from shallowness. I am sure if the Church is to remain a real Society and not be swallowed up in human Society it must be secured in a far deeper grasp of Christ's Cross on the lines you serve so well."

PERCY C. AINSWORTH

Threshold Grace   Meditations in the Psalms.

16mo, cloth, net 50c.

"A very delightful and helpful new volume of meditations in the Psalms, full of devotional reflections for the quiet hour, which make a personal appeal to every Christian man or woman. It is a very well wrought out book of devotion, and pleasing and readable throughout."—*Herald and Presbyter.*

S. D. GORDON

The Consummation of Calvary

Its Foreshadowings, Facts and Spirit.

Idyll Envelope Series, net 25c.

"Mr. Gordon presents the subject with remarkable skill and penetration and the publishers have really outdone themselves in presenting this charming booklet."
—*California Christian Advocate.*

WILLIAM EDWARD BIEDERWOLF

A Help to the Study of the Holy Spirit

New Edition. 12mo, cloth, net 75c.

"Especially clear and valuable is the chapter on the 'Filling of the Spirit.' This seems to me one of the best presentations of the meaning of this great scriptural phase I have ever read."—*Prof. Henry Goodwin Smith, Lane Theological Seminary.*

DEVOTIONAL

ROBERT F. HORTON

The Triumphant Life: Life, Warfare and Victory through the Cross

16mo, Cloth, net 50c.

The author, one of the most influential preachers and devotional writers, presents an attractive volume of brief counsels on Faith and Duty.

CHARLES BROWN

Lessons from the Cross

16mo, Cloth, net 50c.

A volume of remarkable spiritual power which will also prove an incentive to further study of this great subject.

MILFORD HALL LYON

For the Life That Now Is

16mo, Cloth, net 75c.

"Emphasizes the power and presence of a life hid with Christ in God. It will be a revelation to many that there is such a correspondence between the needs of mankind and the provisions of redeeming grace."—*Reformed Church Messenger.*

HANNAH WHITALL SMITH

The Christian's Secret of a Happy Life

New Edition, with Decorative Lace Border and Lace Cover Design. 12mo, Cloth, net $1.00.

A Handsome New Gift Edition of this famous Christian classic, which as a prominent writer once said will "transform the dark days of your life, as it has transformed those of thousands before you."

J. H. JOWETT

Our Blessed Dead

16mo, Boards, 25c.

A booklet of consolation; suggestive and effective.

CORTLAND MYERS

The Real Holy Spirit

12mo, Cloth, net 50c.

"To make this unreality real and mighty in the life of the individual and of the Church is the purpose of this book, that is eminently sane and practical, and will appeal with force to every thoughtful and earnest Christian."—*Christian Guardian.*

CHARLES G. TRUMBULL

Messages for the Morning Watch

Devotional Studies in Genesis. 12mo, cloth, net $1.00.

The value of these morning messages from the pen of the editor of *The Sunday School Times* will be found in their practical application to everyday Christian living. Evidently written out of a heart experience in connection with devout personal study, they throb with life.

PROF. J. SHERMAN WALLACE

The Real Imitation of Christ

12mo, cloth, net 75c.

The purpose of the book is to convince the youth of to-day that to imitate the Christ life is both possible and desirable. Each distinguishing moral characteristic of Jesus is presented in a separate chapter. As a leader of young people's work and a teacher of youth the author possesses both the ability and experience needed to arrest and hold the attention of the young reader. There is a dynamic power in these chapters that will generate in the mind of the reader a strong desire to imitate the great example.

EVAN HOPKINS

Broken Bread for Daily Use

32mo, cloth, net 50c.   Limp leather, gilt edge, net, $1.

The author who is editor of "The Life of Faith" has taken for his every day comment the "head line texts" in that most popular of devotional aids, "Daily Light on the Daily Path." The result is a very unusual little guide to spiritual thinking which will bring inspiration and uplift for each new day.

ANDREW MURRAY

The State of the Church

A Plea for More Prayer. 12mo, cloth, net 75c.

Dr. Murray deplores the lack of spiritual vigor in the churches and believes the chief cause is a decline in the prayer life of the individual. The book constitutes a stirring appeal to the Church to inaugurate a period of deeper consecration and prayer. This the author shows is essential before truly aggressive and effective missionary work, both at home and abroad, can be done.

ENOCH E. BYRUM

The Secret of Prayer

Suggestions How to Pray. 12mo, cloth, net $1.00.

A most devotional as well as evangelical study of prayer together with suggestions as to how best to pray.